AF576420

Monet at Vétheuil | THE TURNING POINT

The University of Michigan Museum of Art
Ann Arbor, Michigan
January 25–March 15, 1998

Dallas Museum of Art
Dallas, Texas
March 28–May 17, 1998

Minneapolis Institute of Arts
Minneapolis, Minnesota
May 30–July 26, 1998

Monet at Vétheuil | THE TURNING POINT

Annette Dixon

Carole McNamara

Charles Stuckey

ISBN 0-912303-52-2

Library of Congress Catalog
Card Number 94-12045

Copyright © 1998 by The Regents
of the University of Michigan
Laurence B. Deitch, Bloomfield Hills
Daniel D. Horning, Grand Haven
Olivia P. Maynard, Goodrich
Shirley M. McFee, Battle Creek
Rebecca McGowan, Ann Arbor
Andrea Fischer Newman, Ann Arbor
Philip H. Power, Ann Arbor
S. Martin Taylor, Grosse Pointe Farms
Lee C. Bollinger, *ex officio*

This exhibition would not have been possible without the generous support of the following organizations:

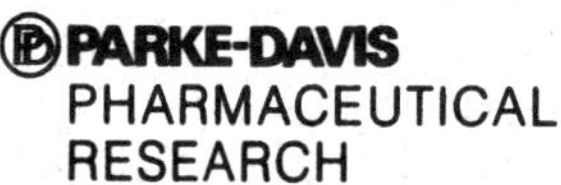

DykemaGossett PLLC

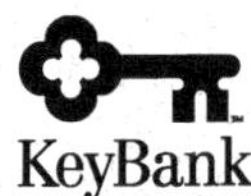

Masco Corporation

Beacon Investment Company

Edward Surovell Realtors
GM Powertrain
The University of Michigan
The City of Ann Arbor

This exhibition is supported by an indemnity from the Federal Council on the Arts and the Humanities.

Cover
Claude Monet, *La Débâcle (The Breakup of the Ice)*, detail, 1880, W. 565, University of Michigan Museum of Art, Ann Arbor. Acquired through the generosity of Mr. Russell B. Stearns (LS&A, 1916) and his wife, Andrée B. Stearns, Dedham, Massachusetts, 1976/2.134.

Inside cover
A map of Vétheuil from 1900, detail. Cartothèque IGN, Paris.

Designed by Mike Savitski,
Ann Arbor, Michigan

Printed by University Lithoprinters, Inc.,
Ann Arbor, Michigan

CONTENTS

Lending Institutions

Ann Arbor, University of Michigan Museum of Art

Bern, Kunstmuseum Bern

Dallas, Dallas Museum of Art

Dunedin, New Zealand, Dunedin Public Art Gallery

Madrid, Fundación Colección Thyssen-Bornemisza

Minneapolis, Minneapolis Institute of Arts

New York, The Metropolitan Museum of Art

Paris, Musée Marmottan

Paris, Musée d'Orsay

Toronto, Art Gallery of Ontario

The permanent collection of the University of Michigan Museum of Art includes a painting by Claude Monet, *La Débâcle*, showing the breakup of the ice along the Seine river in January of 1880. The painting was the inspiration for a graduate seminar and subsequent exhibition in 1979, *The Crisis of Impressionism*, organized by university faculty member Professor Joel Isaacson. This painting has once again served as a catalyst for an exhibition. The present exhibition is the third in a series of exhibitions, entitled *In Focus*, that examine one work from the permanent collection, gathering related objects that can provide an understanding of the work that is both broader in context and greater in depth. Professor Emeritus Isaacson's enthusiasm for this exhibition in the initial planning stages helped spur the project on. Annette Dixon and I are both grateful for his invaluable counsel. Our heartfelt thanks go also to Dr. Charles Stuckey, who authored one of the catalogue essays. His many conversations with us throughout the writing of the catalogue helped hone the essays in focus and substance, and contributed toward a satisfying collaboration among the three authors. Thanks are also due to former director William J. Hennessey, who proposed the *In Focus* series of exhibitions and suggested that we consider organizing an exhibition featuring our Monet. His encouragement and support helped make this exhibition a success.

Monet at Vétheuil: The Turning Point focuses on a little-known period of Monet's career, the few years that he spent at Vétheuil, a small town along the Seine that was featured in many of the artist's paintings. The works included in this exhibition display the full range of Monet's subject matter, some of it quite familiar, and some much less so: summer landscapes along the river, two of his infrequent still-life paintings, several of the paintings of the frozen Seine and subsequent thaw, and only one figure painting, the exceptional deathbed portrait of his first wife, Camille. A number of these paintings have never been exhibited in the United States before. It attests to the importance of the exhibition's focus on this understudied period that the lenders were so graciously willing to part with their paintings for the duration of the exhibition.

When Claude Monet installed himself and his family at Vétheuil in August of 1878, he wrote to his friend Eugène Murer that he had "pitched his tent along the shores of the Seine at Vétheuil, in a ravishing spot." The three turbulent years he spent there were filled with trials and challenges: financial, personal, and artistic. However, as he assured Murer in the same letter of September 1, he expected to do some "not bad things." The paintings included in this exhibition demonstrate that Monet's

Vétheuil works represented a watershed for the artist. As you will read in the essays in this catalogue, Monet's trials and challenges at Vétheuil yielded new ways of working and living. Reconstituting his family along the Seine, and joining it with that of Alice Hoschedé, who was to become his second wife, Monet responded creatively to a remarkable meteorological event, and experimented with a serial approach that was to become the hallmark of his later work. These works from Vétheuil, largely bypassed in favor of Monet's more familiar paintings of Argenteuil and Giverny, can be seen as signaling a major shift in his artistic production and method of exhibition.

Carole McNamara
Interim Director
University of Michigan Museum of Art

ACKNOWLEDGMENTS

Every loan exhibition is a collaboration; only with the help of many people, both within the organizing institution, and from outside, do such exhibitions become successes. This project has benefited from the contributions of many individuals. Of those whose contributions were essential to the realization of the exhibition, we would like first to thank University of Michigan Vice Provost for the Arts and Dean of the School of Music Paul Boylan. His support for and commitment to the presentation of the exhibition were critical during a transitional year at the Museum. His faith in the Museum and its staff is warmly acknowledged by all of us at the Museum. The other person whose early and continuous support played a major role in the exhibition is Helmut Stern. We extend our deep appreciation not only for his counsel, but also for his generous contribution in support of this catalogue.

We are grateful to the members of the staff at each lending institution who generously assisted our efforts and who made possible the loan of works in their collections: Hans Christoph von Tavel and Sandor Kuthy at the Kunstmuseum Bern, Bern; John McCormack and John Timmons at the Dunedin Public Art Gallery, Dunedin, New Zealand; Julian Leon, Tomás Lloréns, and Marianna Aparicio at the Fundación Colección Thyssen-Bornemisza, Madrid; Arnaud de Hauterives and Marianne Delafond at the Musée Marmottan, Paris; Henri Loyrette and Caroline Mathieu at the Musée d'Orsay, Paris; Maxwell L. Anderson, Matthew Teitelbaum, Michael Parke-Taylor, and Barry

Simpson at the Art Gallery of Ontario, Toronto; Jay Gates, Charles L. Venable, Dorothy Kosinski, Debra Wittrup, and Gabriella Truly at the Dallas Museum of Art, Dallas; Evan Maurer, Charles Stuckey (now at the Kimbell Art Museum, Fort Worth), Laura DeBiaso, and Peggy Tolbert at the Minneapolis Institute of Arts, Minneapolis; and Philippe de Montebello, Gary Tinterow, and Nestor Montilla at the Metropolitan Museum of Art, New York.

We would like to thank the following staff members at various research institutions who have helped us in our research: Myriam Favre at the Organisation Météorologique Mondiale, Geneva; Madame Canterel Besson at the Archives du Musée du Louvre, Paris; Eric de Lussy at the Bibliothèque de l'Institut de France, Paris; M. Pelletier at the Bibliothèque Nationale, Paris; Jean-Claude Dupuis at the Institut Géographique National, Paris; Daniel Wildenstein and Michèle Paret at the Institut Wildenstein, Paris, and Ay-Whang Hsia at Wildenstein and Company, New York; Chantal Vimpère at Météo-France, Paris; Monsieur Gerhart at the Service de la Navigation, Limay; Francine Ozanne at the Société Géologique de France, Paris; Keith Seitter at the American Meteorological Society, Boston; Robert E. Parks at The Pierpont Morgan Library, New York. The staff at the following institutions provided invaluable help: the Bibliothèque d'Art et d'Archéologie (Fondation Jacques Doucet), Paris; the Bibliothèque Nationale, Paris; the Bibliothèque Historique de la Ville de Paris, Paris; Roger-Viollet, Paris; and the Interlibrary Loan office of the University of Michigan Libraries.

Special thanks are owed to many individuals for their help in various aspects of the exhibition and this catalogue. Joel Isaacson provided advice very early on in the project. Colin Bailey was responsible for helpful consultation. Joachim Pissarro was enthusiastic about our enterprise from the beginning. Grace Seiberling and Paul Tucker helped shape the direction that the project eventually took. Janet Whitmore assisted with proofreading. Christopher Campbell and Nancy Locke provided background information on the town of Vétheuil. At the University of Michigan Alina Clej, John D'Arms, Raymond Grew, Roberta Hardy, Dennis Kahlbaum, Howard Lay, Marcel Muller, Paul Seelbach, and Paul Webb were instrumental in helping us extend the scope of our inquiries. Claude A. Bonvalot, Mayor of Moisson, and MM. Arnaud Ramière de Fortanier and Olivier Mijoint from the Archives Départementales des Yvelines were wonderful resources concerning the history of the Seine in the vicinity of Vétheuil. In Paris Michel Rostand kindly granted permission to consult his thesis at the Archives du Musée du Louvre. J. Theodore Johnson, Jr. of the University of Kansas, Lawrence, provided insight into Proust's references to Monet. Kenneth Katz of Conservation and Museum Services and James Wright of the Museum of Fine Arts, Boston, gave us pertinent information relating to the varnishing of Monet's paintings.

Staff of the University of Michigan Museum of Art helped in numerous ways. We would like to thank the following: for reading this manuscript, James Manheim; for graphic design, Mike Savitski, Anjali Mehta, and Susan Thompson; for photography, Patrick Young; for registrarial assistance, Lori Mott and Charles Croslin; for computer expertise, Antonia Kramer and David Erdody; for preparation and installation, Kevin Canze, Kirsten Neelands, and Mark Nielsen; for administrative assistance, Kathryn Huss and Jo Lau; for guidance with the budget, Terri Gable; for development, Kathleen Vakalo; for coordinating volunteers, Diana Sepac; for publicity and public relations, Whitley Hill; for family programs and special events, Michelle Burkhead and Karen Ganiard; for Museum shop sales and ticketing, Suzanne Witthoff; and for security, Richard Crowley, Wayne Kilbourn, Thomas Walsh, Xu Yong, and Stanley Zulch. Special thanks are owed to Frances Wylie for organizing the activities of the Friends and to Gail Morawa and Suzan Alexander for organizing Monet-related Friends' trips. In particular, we wish to acknowledge an inestimable debt of gratitude to Rachel Vez Fridrich for help in the research for this project and in the preparation of this catalogue; without her dedication and many thousands of hours of hard work this enterprise would have nearly impossible.

Within the Museum many volunteers helped to enrich the exhibition through hours of dedicated service. The Museum of Art's docent corps has provided special tours of the exhibition and has made a significant contribution to making the exhibition accessible to visitors of all ages. Thanks are also due to the many other volunteers who have augmented our efforts both before and during the run of the exhibition. Of special note in this effort is the Board of the Friends of the Museum, whose creativity and energy were of inestimable assistance in the planning of the exhibition's events: Frances Wylie, President, Suzan Alexander, Thomas Bartlett, Phil Cole, Dorothy Farhat, Eden Gallon, Jane Hann, Melanie Hoff, Howard King, Christine Larson, Gail Morawa, Constance Osler, Julie Rivard, Meeyung Schmitter, Lara Schock, Herbert Sloan, Sara Thornton, Marcine Westerman, and Ralph Youngren.

The project benefited from the support of a number of sources within the University of Michigan. We would like to thank the Office of the President, the Office of the Provost, the Office of the Vice President for Research, the School of Music, the Horace H. Rackham School of Graduate Studies, and the School of Business Administration for their generous support of the exhibition. For grants that were of critical importance to the project at several stages, we would like to thank the Office of the Vice President for Research, the College of Literature, Science & the Arts, and the International Institute.

Numerous organizations and members of the community assisted in various ways toward the success of this endeavor. The mayor of Ann Arbor, Ingrid Sheldon, and the Blue Ribbon committee of community leaders that she assembled were integral to the exhibition's success. We thank Ingrid Sheldon, Mayor, Bruce Benner, Margaret and Timothy Connors, Jean and Tom Dickinson, Deanna Dorner, Patricia Garcia, Elwood Holman, Edward Hood, Mary Kerr, Howard King, Liz Nowland-Margolis, Ron Miller, Judy and Mike Nold, Karen Koykka O'Neal, Michele and Thomas Richardson, Ted Schwarz, Jorge Solis, Edward Surovell, Carroll Walterhouse, and David Wierman.

It is with deep gratitude that we acknowledge the support of our sponsors Dykema Gossett, KeyBank, Masco Corporation, NBD Bank, Beacon Investment Co., Edward Surovell Realtors, and GM Powertrain. This exhibition would not have been possible without their support.

We also recognize the Ann Arbor Area Convention and Visitors Bureau, the Ann Arbor Transportation Authority, the Ann Arbor News, the Ann Arbor Observer, the Ann Arbor Chamber of Commerce, Briarwood Mall, Goetzcraft Printers, Inc., Mitchell Home Medical, Q Ltd., Mildred R. Hartsook, Professor and Mrs. Arnold Kluge, and Dean James W. Richards for their contributions.

Without the enthusiastic support of these University, community, and corporate benefactors this exhibition would never have been possible.

Carole McNamara
Interim Director
University of Michigan
Museum of Art

Annette Dixon
Curator of Western Art
University of Michigan
Museum of Art

Charles Stuckey
Senior Curator
Kimbell Art Museum

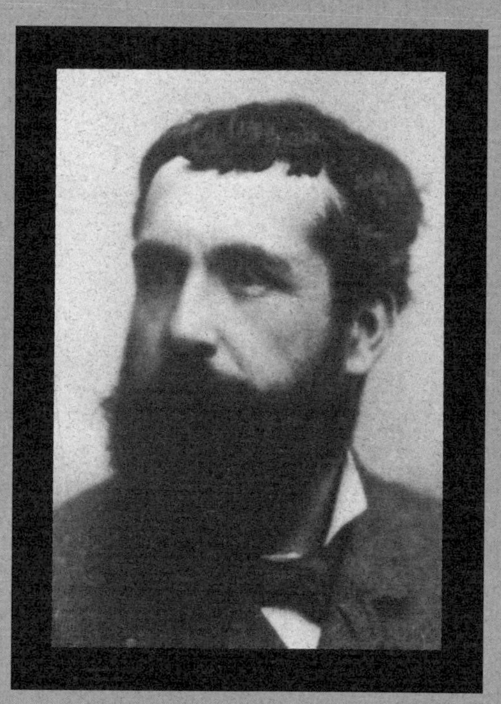

Schaarwachter

Portrait of Claude Monet

Ca. 1880

Albumen print

folio 2, #326

Bibliothèque Historique de la Ville de Paris

Introduction

While Monet's work has been the focus of many exhibitions and monographs in recent years, these studies have not fully examined his Vétheuil period—a decisive moment of personal and artistic reassessment during which the artist experimented with serial painting, a mode that was to dominate his later work. The exhibition *Monet at Vétheuil: The Turning Point* demonstrates that the years 1878-1881, which Monet spent in Vétheuil, were of crucial importance to his artistic development. This was a time of artistic catharsis during which Monet overcame deep professional self-doubt and complicated personal difficulties. From this crisis the artist forged a fresh direction in his art, chiefly by experimenting with rendering the landscape, which laid the groundwork for his subsequent serial approach. Through the ensemble of paintings generally referred to as the *Débâcles*, his other scenes at Vétheuil, still lifes, and the portrait of the artist's deceased wife, Camille, the exhibition demonstrates that the *Débâcles* must be seen as a true turning point for the artist.

Vétheuil's Place in Monet's Career

The years immediately preceding Monet's move to Vétheuil saw him celebrated as one of the major painters of modern life. The classic Impressionist paintings from Argenteuil in the early and mid-1870s reflect Monet's concerns with both urban and suburban subject matter, including leisure pursuits and daily activities. It was at Vétheuil that the artist abandoned these contemporary themes for the fugitive aspects of nature in his landscape painting. There, almost for the first time with the *Débâcle* paintings, he grappled with the vagaries of the weather as they affected a specific topographical site. Within several years of leaving Vétheuil, he settled at Giverny, where his garden provided a virtually inexhaustible set of motifs for him to explore.

The years 1878-1881 were to prove pivotal in Monet's life and career, and we can chart the change in his artistic fortunes through the shifts in the manner in which he exhibited his works, with resulting critical and financial success. He also redirected his subject matter, eliminating modernity and concentrating on nature and the landscape, in particular in his *Débâcles*, the impressive series of paintings that emerged from the severe cold and flood during the winter of 1879-1880. In this group of about twenty paintings on the subject of the thaw of the frozen Seine and in other views of sites around Vétheuil, Monet conceived his paintings in pairs, triplets, or larger groupings. He varied viewpoints, times of day, and qualities of light and atmosphere.

Catalogue Essays

The three essays that follow explore different facets of Monet's years at Vétheuil. In the first essay Charles Stuckey, Senior Curator at the Kimbell Art Museum in Fort Worth, Texas, examines Monet's career through the years leading up to the move to Vétheuil, exploring Monet's commercial relationships with his dealers. He also provocatively reconsiders Monet's unusual relationship with the Hoschedé family.

The second essay, by Carole McNamara, Interim Director at the University of Michigan Museum of Art, looks at the shift in Monet's subject matter following his arrival in Vétheuil and the manner in which Vétheuil and the town across the river, Lavacourt, are depicted. She also describes the effect of the harsh winter of 1879-1880 through an examination of its portrayal in the Paris press, and how Monet's own *Débâcle* paintings relate to those images in the periodicals of the time.

In the third essay Annette Dixon, Curator of Western Art at the University of Michigan Museum of Art, discusses Monet's partial rejection at the Salon of 1880 and his one-man exhibition at *La Vie Moderne*, the latter acting as a catalyst to reverse Monet's critical and financial fortunes. She also challenges the notion of Monet's involvement, at the time of the *Vie Moderne* show, in the formulation of a myth about his creation of paintings exclusively out-of-doors.

Monet finally left Vétheuil for Poissy in 1881, settling permanently at Giverny not long after that. Twenty years later, the artist made one final visit to the area to paint Vétheuil. In the summer and early fall of 1901, having recently purchased a new automobile, he made afternoon excursions to Lavacourt from Giverny. There, from a balcony in Lavacourt, he painted fifteen square canvases of the town where he had lived, apparently without ever crossing over to Vétheuil itself.

PLATES

Note to the Reader

In this catalogue all dimensions are given in centimeters with height preceding width.

All twelve plates reproduce oil paintings on canvas.

No substantive discussion of Monet's work could exist without the excellent catalogue raisonné by Daniel Wildenstein, of which there are two versions (five volumes, Lausanne, 1974-1991; four volumes, Cologne, 1996). Throughout this catalogue Monet's paintings will be referred in the usual manner, i.e., "W." followed by the number in Wildenstein's catalogue.
All translations are by the authors unless otherwise indicated.

PLATE 1

LA DÉBÂCLE

(The Breakup of the Ice)

1880

W. 571

61 x 100 cm

Kunstmuseum Bern, Bern, Legat Eugen Loeb 1960

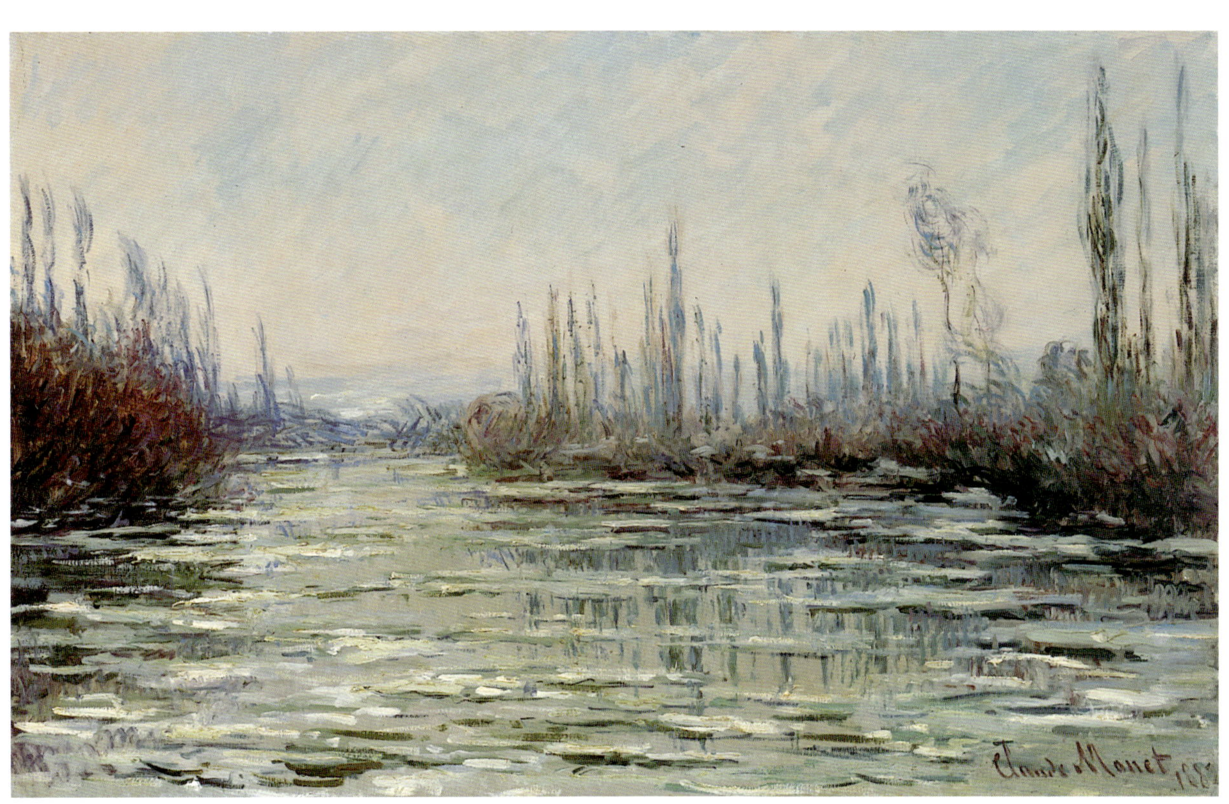
Claude Monet

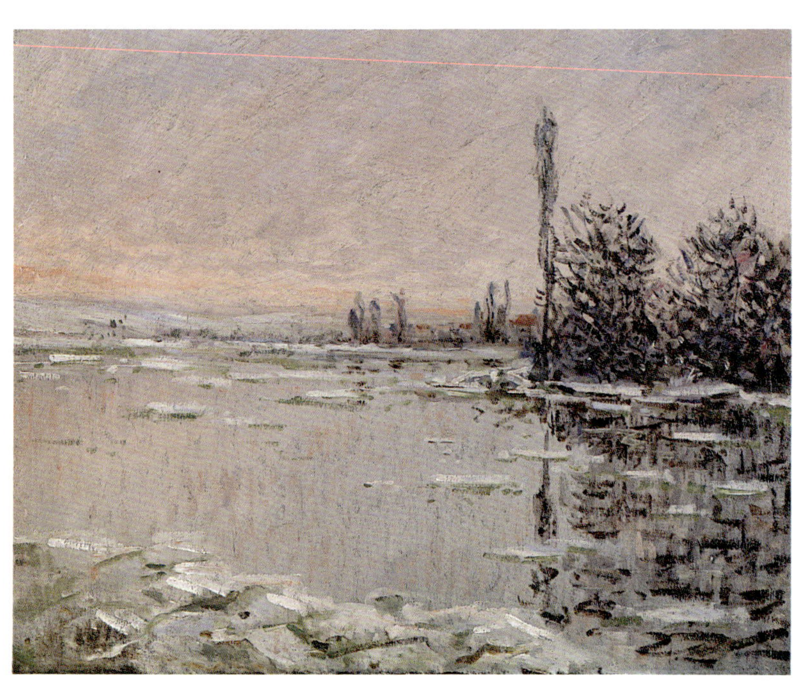

PLATE 2

La Débâcle

(The Breakup of the Ice)

1880

W. 562

54 x 65 cm

Dunedin Public Art Gallery, Dunedin, New Zealand

Given by Mary, Dora, and Esmond de Beer
through the National Art-Collections Fund, 1982

PLATE 3

La Débâcle

(The Breakup of the Ice)

1880

W. 565

60 x 99 cm

University of Michigan Museum of Art, Ann Arbor

Acquired through the generosity of Mr. Russell B. Stearns (LS&A, 1916) and his wife, Andrée B. Stearns, Dedham, Massachusetts, 1976/2.134

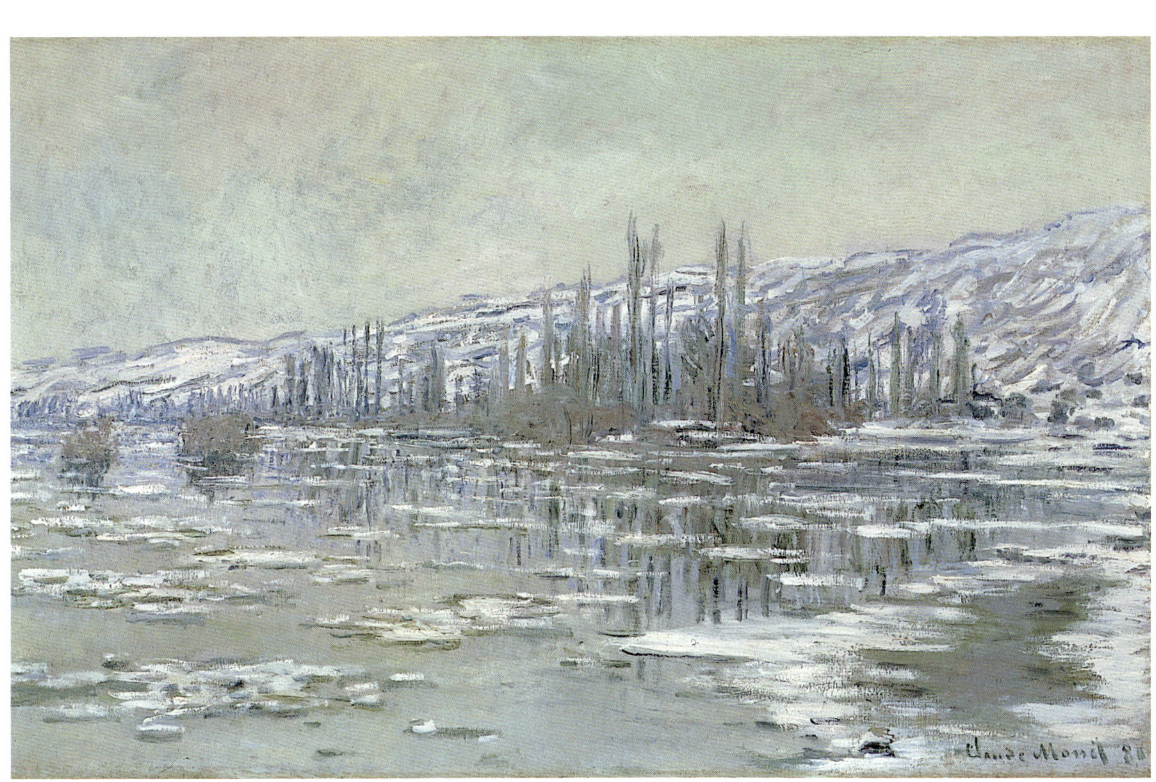

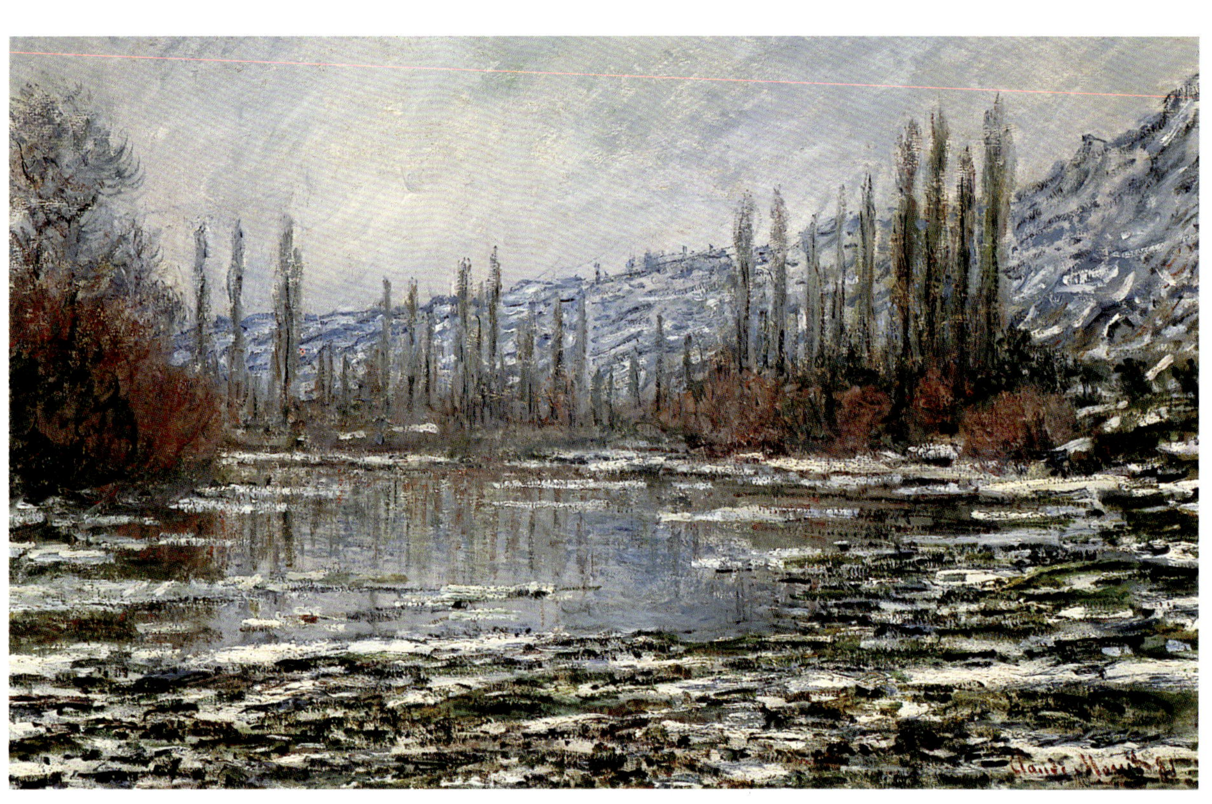

PLATE 4

La Débâcle à Vétheuil

(The Breakup of the Ice at Vétheuil)

1880

W. 566

60 x 100 cm

Fundación Colección Thyssen-Bornemisza, Madrid

PLATE 5

Les Glaçons

(The Ice Floes)

1880

W. 567

61 x 100 cm

Musée d'Orsay, Paris

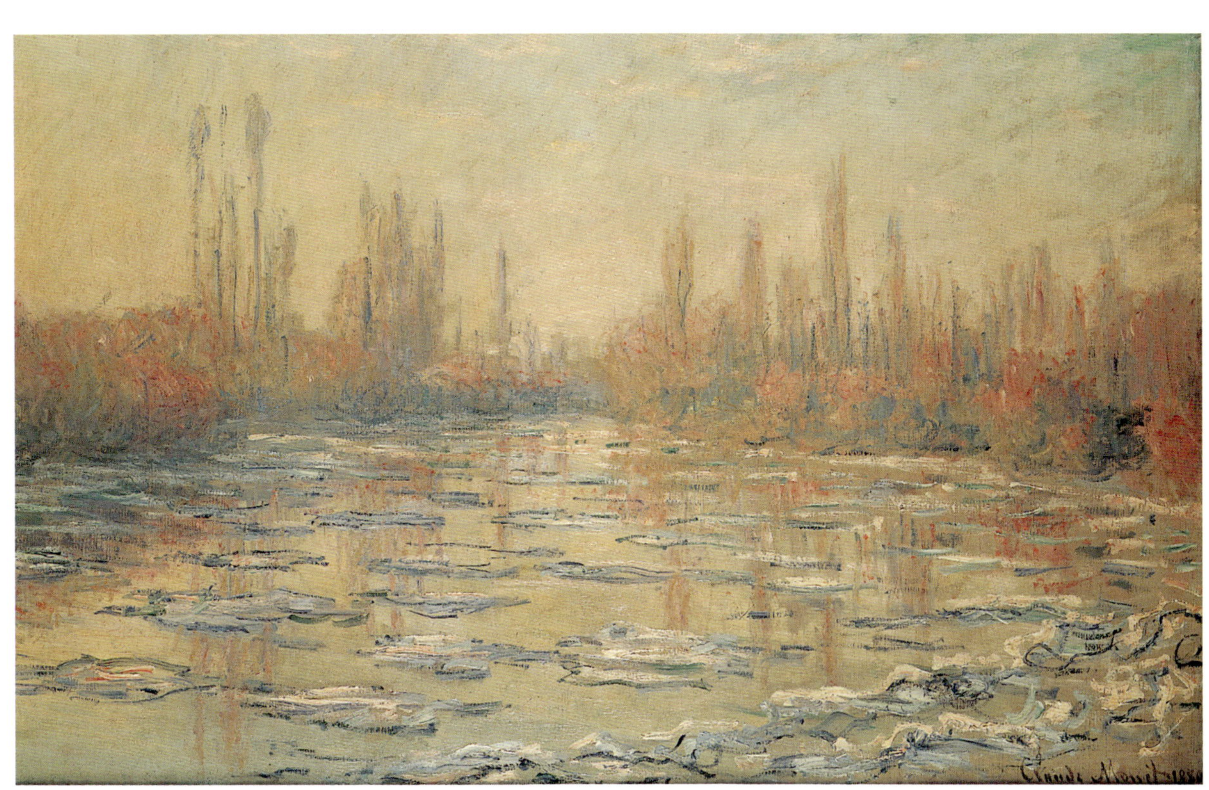

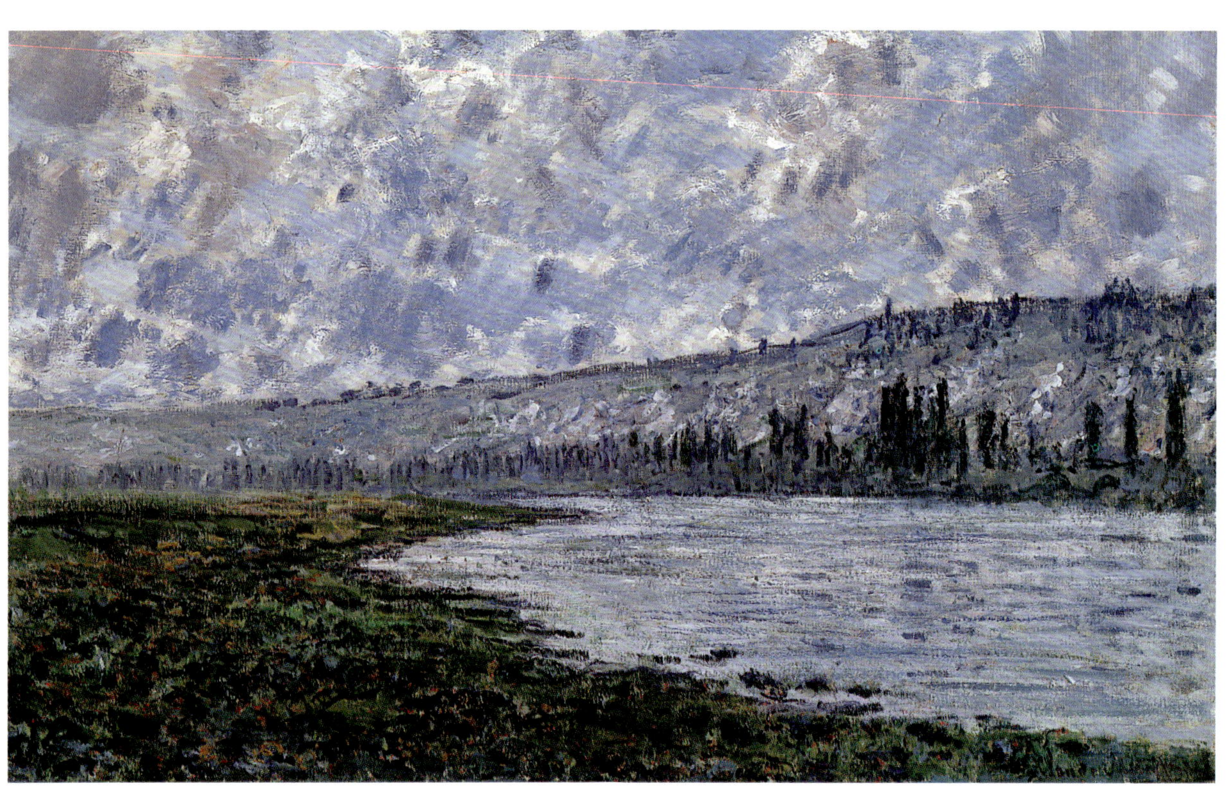

PLATE 6

La Seine à Vétheuil

(The Seine at Vétheuil)

1880

W. 599

60 x 105 cm

The Metropolitan Museum of Art, New York

Theodore M. Davis Collection,

Bequest of Theodore M. Davis, 1915

PLATE 7

LA SEINE À LAVACOURT

(The Seine at Lavacourt)

1880

W. 578

100 x 150 cm

Dallas Museum of Art, Dallas, Munger Fund, 1938.4.M

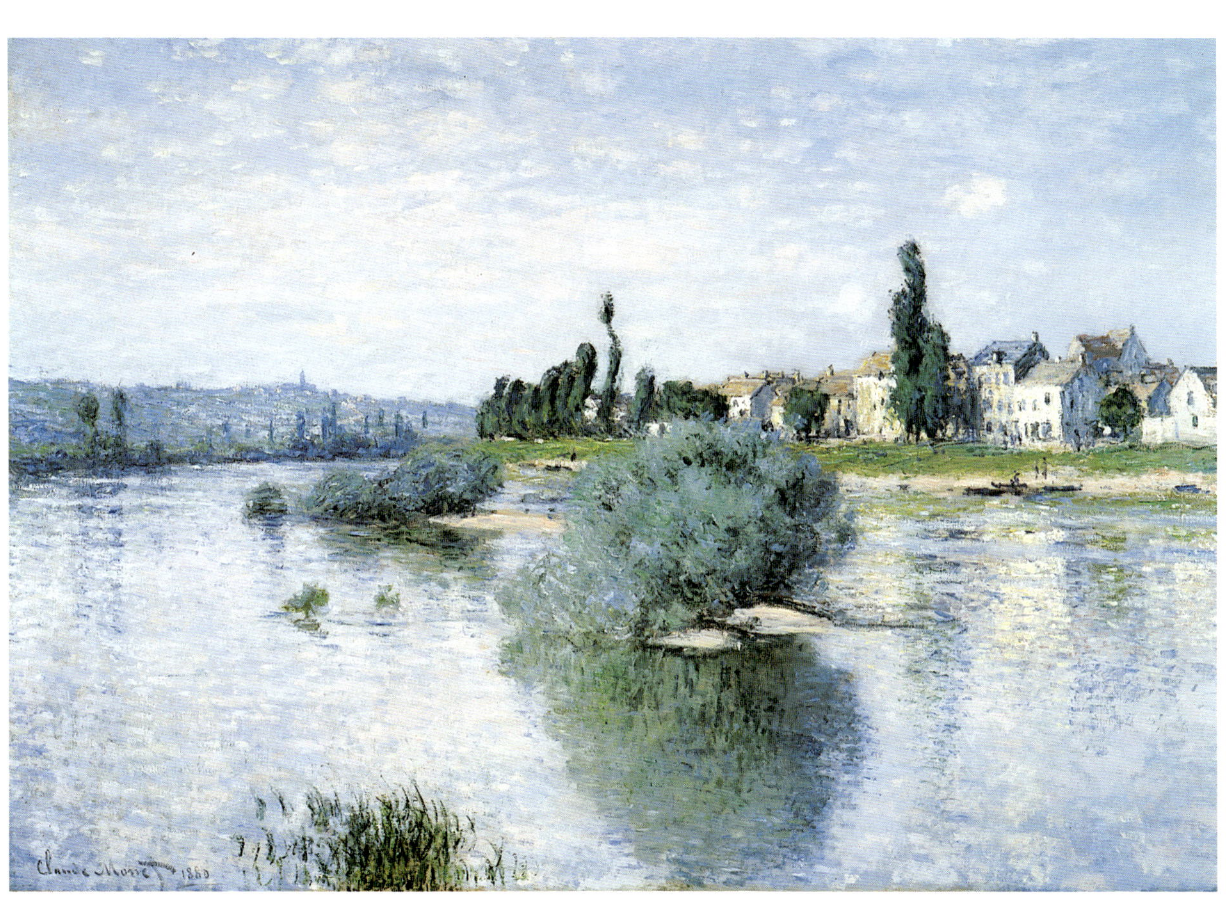

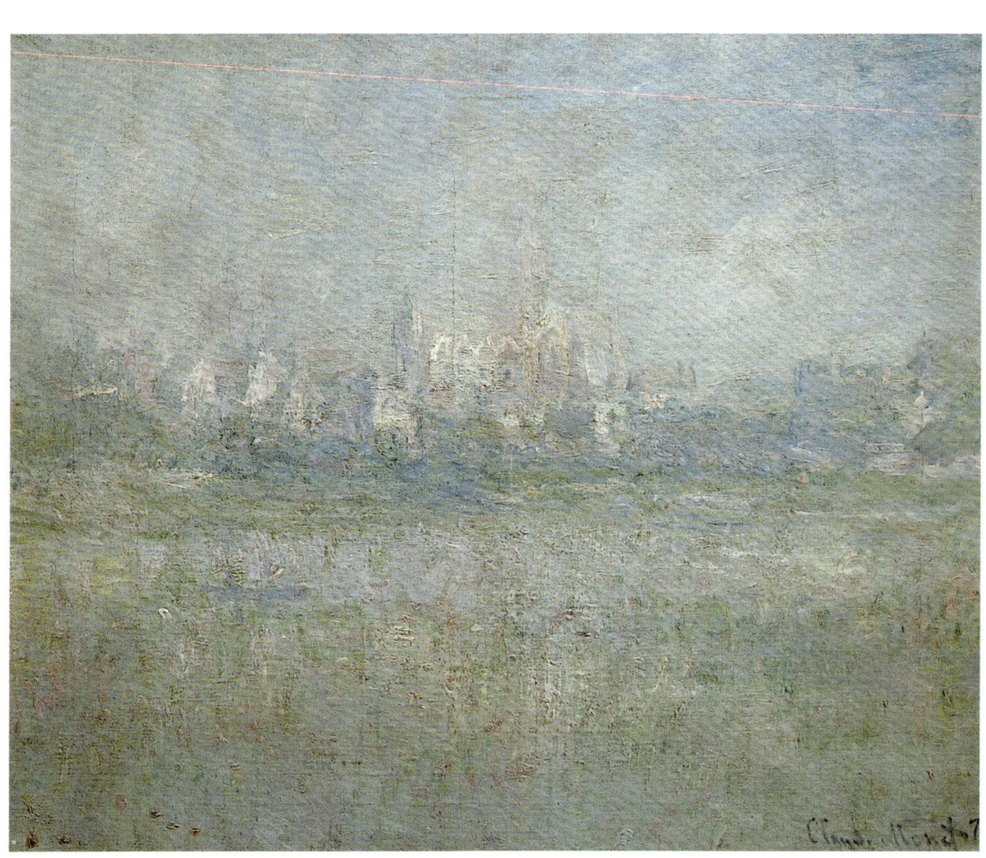

PLATE 8

VÉTHEUIL DANS LE BROUILLARD

(Vétheuil in the Fog)

1879

W. 518

60 x 71 cm

Musée Marmottan, Paris

PLATE 9

VÉTHEUIL EN ÉTÉ

(Vétheuil in Summer)

1879

W. 534

67.7 x 90.5 cm

Art Gallery of Ontario, Toronto

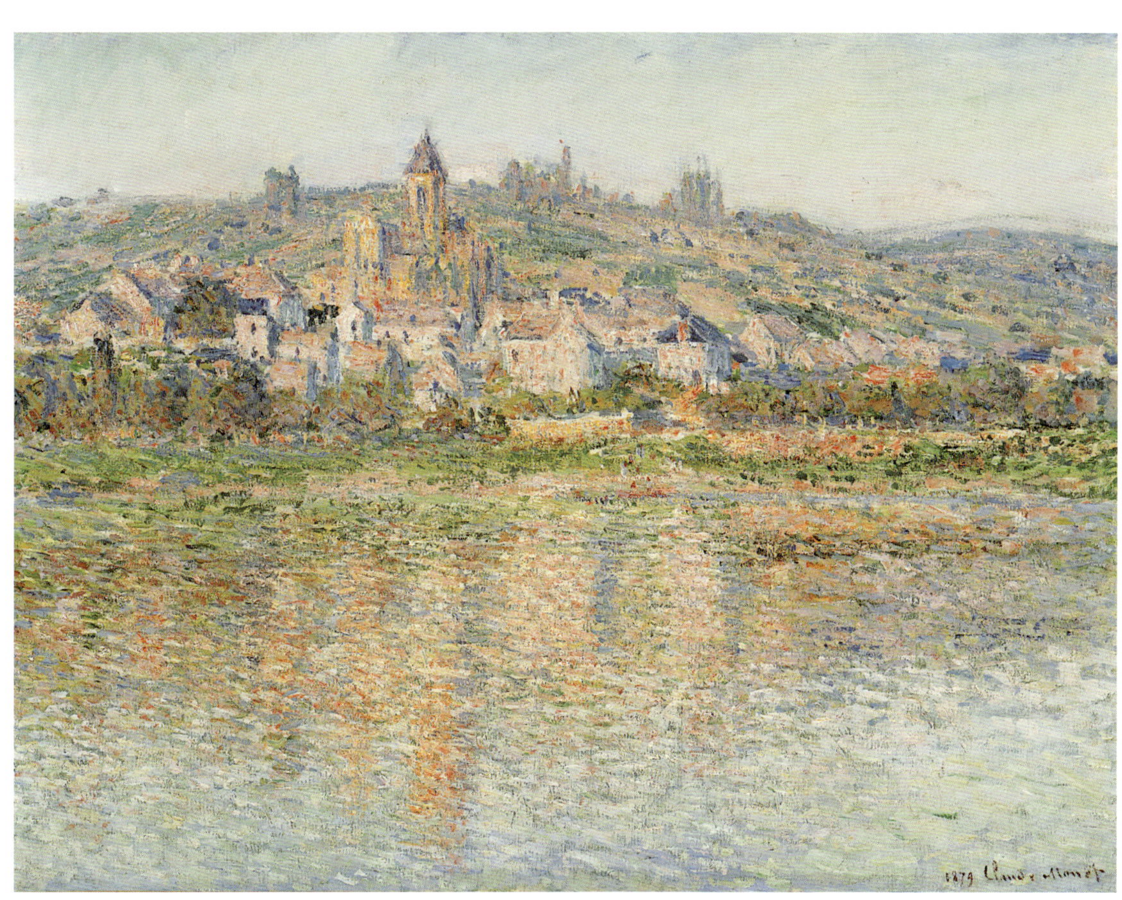
1879 Claude Monet

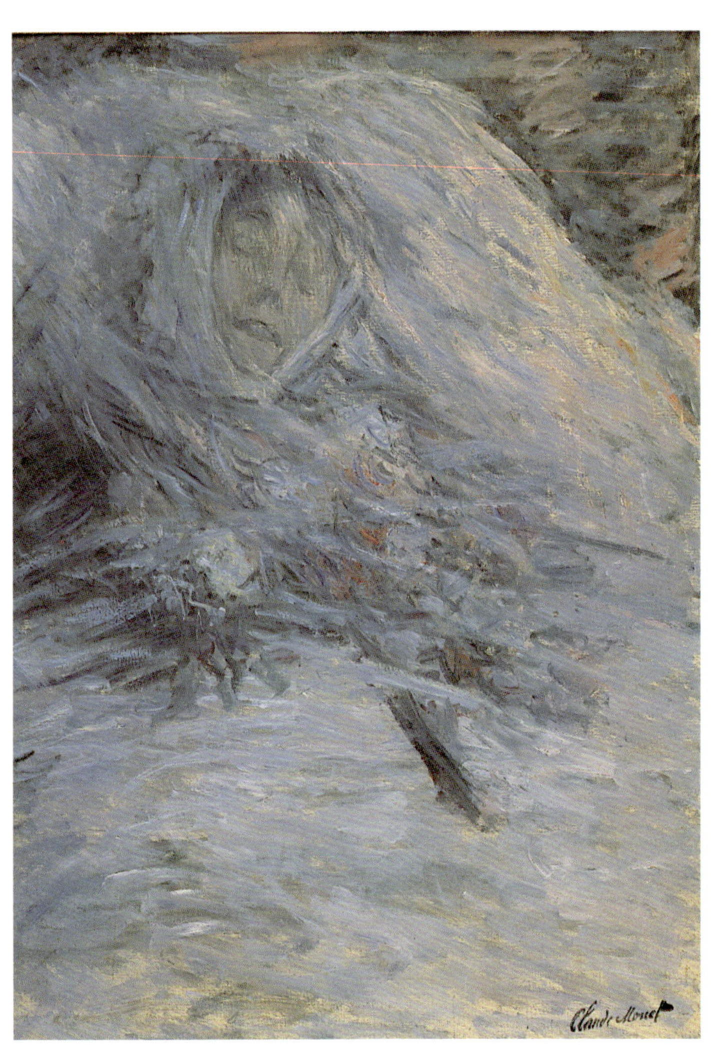
Claude Monet

CAMILLE MONET SUR SON LIT DE MORT

(Camille Monet on Her Deathbed)

1879

W. 543

90 x 68 cm

Musée d'Orsay, Paris

PLATE 11

CORBEILLE DE FRUITS (POMMES ET RAISIN)

(Fruit Basket [Apples and Grapes])

1879

W. 545

68 x 90 cm

The Metropolitan Museum of Art, New York

Gift of Henry R. Luce, 1957

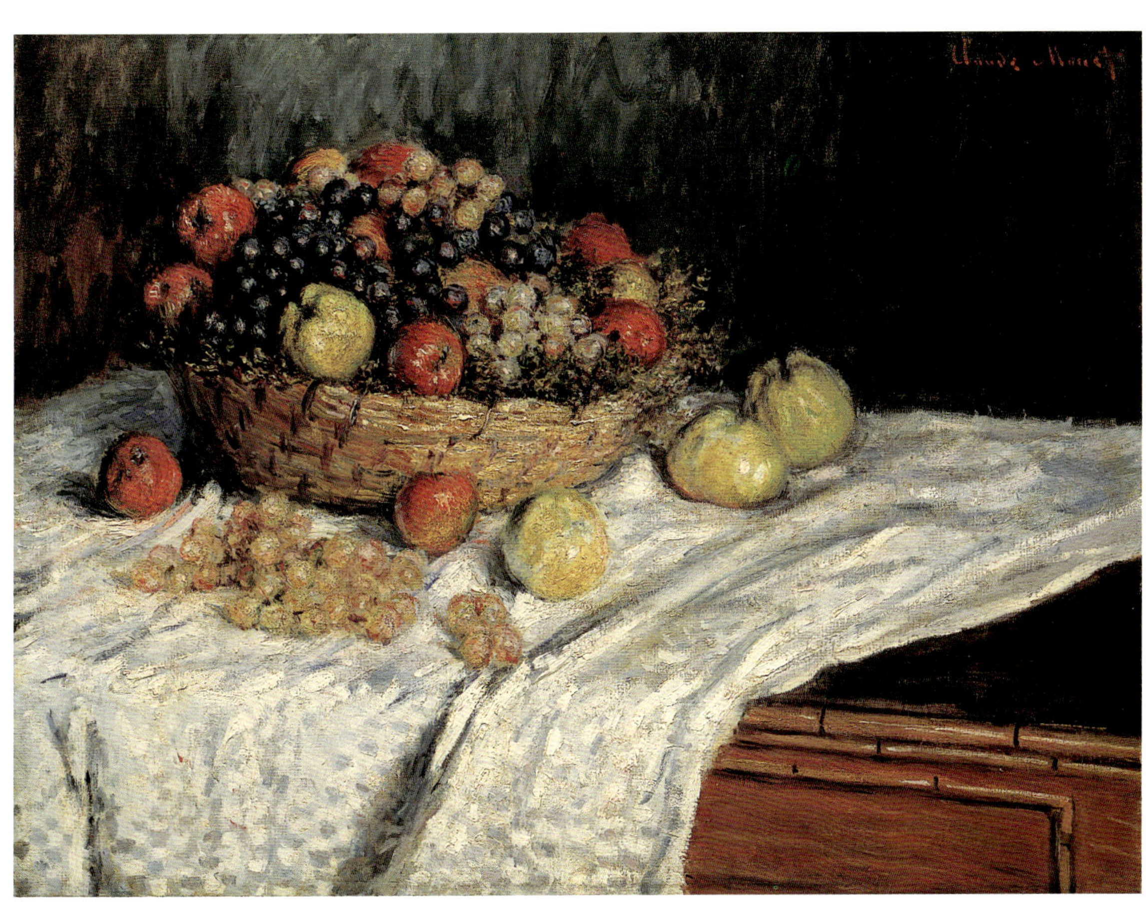
Claude Monet

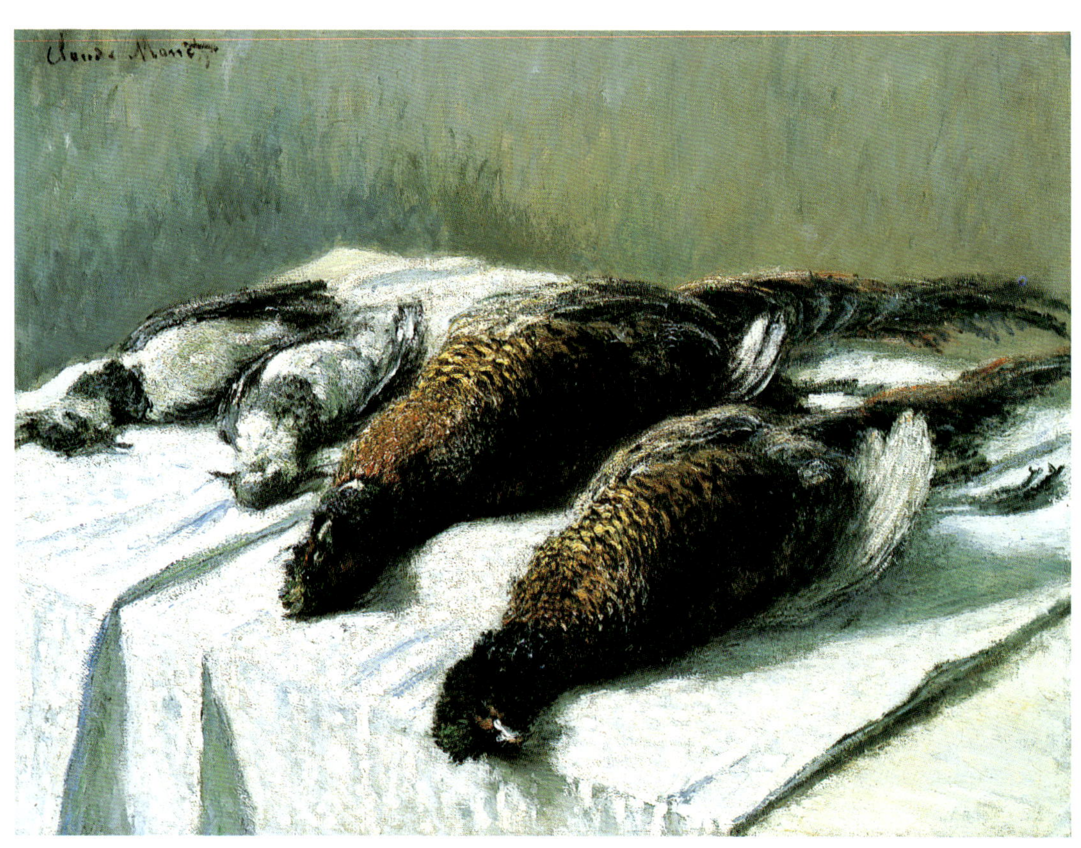
Claude Monet

FAISANS ET VANNEAUX

(Pheasants and Lapwings)

1879

W. 550

68 x 90 cm

The Minneapolis Institute of Arts, Minneapolis

Given by Anne Pierce Rogers in memory of John DeCoster Rogers, 84.140

The most momentous change in the career of the most revolutionary Impressionist painter seems to have come about by chance, if terrible weather can be understood as just one more kind of bad luck. Recording a state of nature that he himself might well have wished to avoid altogether, given the choice, Monet's magnificent January 1880 paintings of the Seine river jammed with blocks of ice, in which daylight reanimates a world all but obliterated in cold, are rather unlike his stock-in-trade of green, sun-brightened landscapes from the previous fifteen or twenty years. True enough, Monet had no choice as an out-of-doors landscape painter during the winter of 1879-1880 but to paint snow and ice, the only subject then at hand. Moreover, it is important to mention that before the winter of 1879-1880 Monet was among the relatively few landscape painters who had mastered winter subjects. He had developed as a sometimes snow-scape artist in response to the Japanese woodblock print masters he so deeply admired, for whom the world blanketed in snow was a subject (*yuki guni*) rich with subtle shapes and closely related tones (see fig. 1), and in response to Gustave Courbet, the great Realist (himself devoted to Japanese art), who dared his European col-

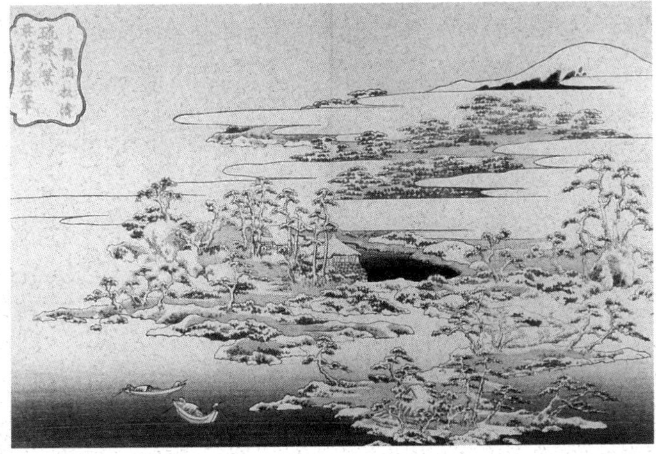

Fig. 1
Katsushika Hokusai
Pines and Waves in Ryudo, the Dragon's Cave. One of the *Eight Views of the Ryukyu Islands*
Ca. 1833
Woodcut
Reproduced by courtesy of the Trustees, British Museum, London

leagues to overcome the physical hardships of painting outside in winter weather (and produced the likes of *Le naufrage dans la neige*, fig. 2). Indeed, Monet during the 1860s and 1870s had found a more favorable market for his snowscapes than might be found for the same works among today's collectors of Impressionism. Today's collectors tend to prefer his classic Impressionist works, which depict the bustle of everyday modern life out-of-doors, with people commuting, gardening, and enjoying other leisure activities. Typical of his pre-1880 paintings, such humankind-in-the-landscape subjects are marginal in his post-1880 output. So, while Monet occasionally painted snowscapes before 1879-1880, his renditions of Vétheuil as a frozen world nevertheless initiate a crucial change in his landscape painting, away from landscape as a stage set for everyday life and towards landscape with little reference to human activity, landscape as a neo-Romantic theater of powerful natural forces. Whether tumultuous in spirit, like those of crashing surf, or meditative, like those of luxuriating water lilies, many of Monet's post-1880 paintings include few signs of human life, aside from cultivated plants. Curiously enough, in terms of compositional patterning, the bunched-together ice blocks on the Seine river in the bleak 1880 *Débâcle* paintings are remarkably similar to the lush display of water-lily pads drifting on the surface of his garden pond in Monet's ultimate works.[1]

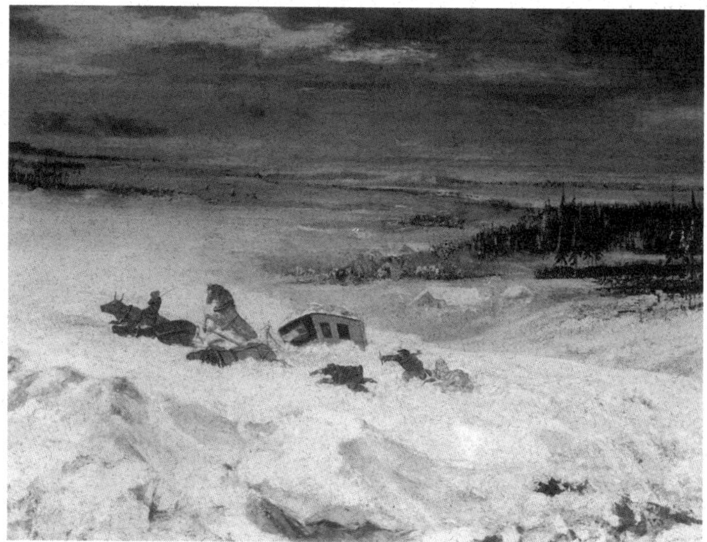

Fig. 2
Gustave Courbet
Le naufrage dans la neige
(Accident in the Snow)
1860
Oil on canvas
Reproduced by courtesy of the Trustees, The National Gallery, London

Except for Monet's last years, when the loss of aging friends and the loss of his own physical powers were overshadowed only by the mass horrors of the First World War, the arctic cold winter of 1879-1880 was arguably more full of personal adversity than any other period of his life. When his wife Camille died in September 1879, leaving him singly responsible for two sons, aged one and twelve, there was scarcely any market demand for his paintings. (Of the little that he could sell, still lifes were seemingly in more demand than any kind of landscape.) It is a wonder that he did not need to find a job aside from painting in order to provide himself and his sons with basic needs. Meanwhile, such important supporters as art critic Émile Zola and collectors Georges de Bellio and Jean-Baptiste Faure now complained that Monet was not carrying his works to a sufficient degree of resolution, implying perhaps some connection to his pathetic hurry to make enough money. And in January 1880 someone (it is too painful to guess who, so nobody ever has) apparently contrived, successfully, to place a newspaper report that Monet had abandoned his principles altogether. A writer going under the name "Tout Paris" in the January 24, 1880, issue of *Le Gaulois* claimed that Monet planned to show his work at the official government exhibition of contemporary art, the annual Salon, rather than participate in the forthcoming private Impressionist exhibition. His decision would mean a betrayal of the efforts Monet had helped to initiate half a dozen years earlier to maintain freedom from mainstream taste in art with independent exhibitions. Worse still, the newspaper writer insinuated that Monet was living shamelessly with the wife of a former associate even less well off than he.[2]

Indeed, Monet now lived in Vétheuil (hardly the easy commute to Paris that his previous suburban home at Argenteuil had provided), where, to cut expenses, he had moved at the end of 1878 together with the family of Ernest Hoschedé, bankrupt Impressionist art collector.[3] While Hoschedé was in Paris on business most of the time, including the business of selling paintings for Monet, his wife, Alice, was "alone" with the painter, except for the combined households' eight children. The very idea that Alice Hoschedé, while she nursed Camille Monet, had been stealing the dying woman's penniless husband is the stuff of Zola's best-selling melodramatic novels. As if in corroboration of the hateful newspaper article, however, by late 1881 the two families moved away from Vétheuil in tandem, prolonging the unusual partnership under the same roof, to Poissy at first, then finally in 1883 to Giverny. When exactly Alice Hoschedé and Monet became lovers, however, is unknown.

Considering the ongoing partnership of Monet and Alice Hoschedé, and their eventual marriage in 1892, the year following Ernest's death, it is now generally believed that Monet and his future second wife had started to have an affair prior to Camille's death.[4] Otherwise, why in the first place would Monet and his family decide to live together with the Hoschedés, of all people, so far outside Paris in Vétheuil? Given the absence of documentation about how the Monets came to be best friends with the Hoschedés in the middle-to-late 1870s, it seems reasonable to wonder why the Monets, when faced with hardships, would not have joined forces instead with such old friends as the Pissarros or the Sisleys. By the time the Monets and Hoschedés installed themselves together in Vétheuil in the autumn of 1878, Camille, who had just given birth the previous March to her second son, Michel, was gravely ill. Given her vulnerability, it would have been cruel for her to be conjoined domestically with unfamiliar people.[5] Is it really plausible that a lustful painter and the lustful wife of a bankrupt collector might conspire to pull the wool over the eyes of their respective families, friends, and neighbors by explaining to them the economic and logistical advantages of merging the two households, by explaining the lack of any other options for either? Would not Camille's longtime friends (for example, Renoir, Manet, the Pissarros, and the Sisleys) have been appalled by such deceit? We can only guess. Indeed, it is not known whether or not such friends came out to Vétheuil for her burial on September 7, 1879. The degree of Monet's abiding affection for Camille is recorded primarily in the deathbed effigy of her that Monet painted. Of course, this work was strictly private, never intended for public exhibition, nor for eventual historical debate. But the fact that Zola, in *L'Oeuvre*, has his painter protagonist paint a comparable deathbed portrait of his child might suggest that the writer, or a mutual friend of his and Monet's, may as a mourner have noticed this final portrayal of Camille during a visit to Vétheuil.[6]

Leaving aside the impact that Camille's death had in the years ahead on Monet's network of old friends, other basic questions need to be asked with respect to the impoverished winter of 1879-1880. How did Monet get himself into poverty in the late 1870s? And then, given his inability to escape financial distress during all those years, how was it that his fortunes suddenly improved in 1880? With whose help? And where had the help been until then? Addressing such questions might involve reconsideration of basic assumptions about the early history of Impressionism.

THROUGH 1870

How far back are the beginnings of the 1879-1880 Monet story? Back as far as 1865, when he started to use Camille Doncieux as a model for the large paintings with which he hoped to win prestige at the vast, heavily attended, government-sponsored contemporary art exhibitions in Paris known as Salons? Or back to 1870, when Monet married her, a woman by now accustomed to hard times on the run with him from creditors and by now mother of their first son, not yet quite three years old? Monet evidently did not yet have any relationship with businessman-collector Ernest Hoschedé, who by 1870 owned a painting by Boudin, Monet's mentor and dear friend of some fifteen years. In October 1870, as Prussian troops advanced unchecked into France, the Monets fled to London, where the artist met fellow exile Paul Durand-Ruel, who had taken over his father's business in selling contemporary art, particularly Barbizon School (School of 1830) landscapes. In a variety of ways still undiscussed in the literature about Impressionism, the meeting of painter and dealer apparently set the stage for how Monet's life and career unfolded during the 1870s and beyond.

Back in Paris after the Franco-Prussian War, Durand-Ruel in 1872 tried to launch Monet's artistic success, buying many of his paintings and showing them (at least in London) alongside works purchased from Degas, Manet, Pissarro, Renoir, and Sisley, as well as works by artists outside of what would become the Impressionist group. Indeed, in his memoirs, Durand-Ruel claims that he also showed Impressionist works at his Paris gallery on the rue Lafitte before 1874, the date of the now historic first Impressionist group exhibition. But the dealer's claim goes unsubstantiated by any as yet uncovered documentation, such as a catalogue checklist or newspaper notice.

Shortly after their return to Paris in late 1871 the Monets had rented a house in the riverside suburb of Argenteuil. It is unknown whether Durand-Ruel took the train out to Argenteuil in 1872 and 1873 to buy paintings or whether he selected works at the studio that Monet kept in Paris, conveniently near the Saint-Lazare train station. Since few of Monet's 1872 or 1873 paintings depict Parisian subjects, however, the artist apparently used his city studio mostly as storeroom and showroom.

At Argenteuil, for the first time in their life together, the Monets enjoyed financial prosperity, thanks to Durand-Ruel, who in 1872 bought works nearly as fast as Monet could paint them. During that year he purchased twenty-nine works from Monet at an average price of about 350 francs each.[7] Simultaneously, Durand-Ruel cornered the market in the works of Manet, Degas, Pissarro, Renoir, and Sisley. Judging from Monet's own notebook record of sales, altogether in 1872 he earned over 12,000 francs, while his annual rent was 1,000 francs for the Argenteuil house and 450 francs for the Paris studio. In 1873, his rent unchanged, Monet sold nearly 25,000 francs' worth of pictures, including thirty-four to Durand-Ruel alone. Monet presumably met Ernest Hoschedé, for this collector began by 1873 to buy paintings from Durand-Ruel, including works by Monet. In a pre-income tax world, Monet's 1872-1873 earnings would have been exceptional, roughly comparable to a gross income today in America of several hundred thousand dollars![8] The fact that the Monets employed two household servants and a gardener would hardly count as overspending. Nor could the boat that Monet bought to use as a mobile studio have strained family finances.

What happened to all that newfound wealth has never been explained. With so much income by 1873, how could Monet have been reduced to asking for small loans as early as 1875, as suggested by his urgent letters in request of money help? Whatever did happen set into motion the complex events that resulted in Monet's move to Vétheuil with the Hoschedés and their interconnected experiences during the brutal winter of 1879-1880. Considering Monet's income through 1872-1873, however, what seems most astonishing is the fact that by early 1873 Monet would take a leading role in the formation of an artists' cooperative designed, it is always assumed, to help controversial painters make more sales. In 1873 these painters, in particular Monet, hardly needed more sales.

LATE 1873 AND PLANS FOR THE FIRST IMPRESSIONIST EXHIBITION IN APRIL 1874

History is the surviving record, partial at best, of what happened, elaborated by hypothetical explanations of why things happened differently from what might have been expected. Although it never yet has, the history of Impressionism should, of course, provide some explanation for why Durand-Ruel himself did not organize and present the first Impressionist exhibition. That would have made sense in 1873, when the dealer, more than anyone, had the capacity and motivation to do so, if the artists only gave their consent.[9] What should history make of the fact that the artists themselves began to consider an independent exhibition by no later than April 1873?[10] Did they make this effort because Durand-Ruel was unwilling to exhibit their works? Or, for some reason, did they prefer to operate independently of Durand-Ruel? It is worth considering whether the painters envied the dealer's commissions on sales and/or feared the possibility that he might accumulate too much inventory power over their future independence in the art market.

Here is Durand-Ruel's own years-after-the-fact account of his remarkable false start as the leading dealer of Impressionism:

> "The first exhibitions of my paintings by Monet, Sisley, Pissarro, Renoir, and Degas that I did [at my] rue Lafitte [gallery] had simply excited curiosity. Most of the visitors looked at [these works] with indifference, but without showing any hostility. A few collectors without prejudice took an interest in them and I had even been able to sell a certain number. The appearance of [the works] that I had bought from Manet and from Puvis de Chavannes was greeted, on the contrary, with a concert of criticism, satire, and insensitive insult. In the wake of absurd articles appearing in certain newspapers, a real campaign of protest was raised against us and soon took on an outrageous and violent character.... In order to ward off the danger that menaced me and most of all thanks to insufficient funds, I had to moderate my purchases, and that is how I allowed my friend Faure, who had a fortune, to replace me where Manet was concerned.... Likewise, he bought a large number of paintings from Monet, Sisley, Pissarro, and Degas. These poor artists, whom I was forced to abandon thanks to circumstances, at least for the moment, were also able to place a few of their works with some of my clients—Hoschedé, Chocquet, the Count Doria, de Bellio, the Hecht brothers, Rouart, Bérard."[11]

Durand-Ruel's account does not check out in its details. As already mentioned, while there are records of Durand-Ruel exhibitions in London with Impressionist paintings, as far as is known he did not exhibit their works in Paris in 1872 and 1873. Nor is there any evidence of virulent press attacks against any works that he had bought from Manet and Puvis de Chavannes. Moreover, Durand-Ruel did not stop buying works by the Impressionists little by little. At least where Monet is concerned, Durand-Ruel stopped his purchases suddenly, after December 9, 1873, only days before Monet and his colleagues officially incorporated themselves on December 27 in order to stage an exhibition, in rooms that they would soon arrange to rent from the photographer Nadar. Although such fears are suggested between the lines of Durand-Ruel's memoirs, it nevertheless seems highly dubious from a business point of view that the dealer, operating with discretion, might risk losing important clients if he continued to obtain Impressionist works for other collectors. After all, then as now, every commission counted.

What caused the sudden suspension (around the 1873 Christmas holidays) of the very active relationship between Durand-Ruel and Monet is unknown. Monet's own sales records for 1873 provide a few details in the otherwise mostly blank historical picture. Having sold works to Durand-Ruel at roughly 350 francs each in 1872, Monet started 1873 with the sale of an 1867 cityscape (W. 85) for 1000 francs to a Mr. Bériot, paid in installments through the year. At that time Bériot could have bought a similar cityscape (W. 84) by Monet from Durand-Ruel, who in June 1872 had bought just such a painting from Zacharie Astruc. In this particular transaction with Bériot did Monet knowingly undersell Durand-Ruel, perhaps to leverage higher wholesale prices or other business concessions from the dealer?

Whatever the case, on February 24, 1873, the dealer selected twenty-five Monet paintings at more elevated prices. Only seven of these were 300-franc paintings; the others, including two snow scenes, sold for 400 and 500 francs. Exceptional was a painting of *La Grenouillère*, from 1869, priced at 2000 by itself. In July 1873 Monet also received 262 francs for one of his works (possibly W. 244) sold at auction in Paris. Although details are vague, evidently Monet himself wished to learn what one of his paintings might bring if floated on the market to the highest bidder.

Durand-Ruel's first recorded sale of a Monet painting to Hoschedé took place in April 1873. How soon Monet learned of the sale is unknown, but in May 1873, he had seemingly established new, elevated pricing ideas. It was then that the contemporary art critic and cognac distributor Théodore Duret decided to buy an 1860s painting (W. 94) from Monet that his friend Manet had seen in Argenteuil for sale at 1200 francs.[12]

The high price range that Monet maintained with this sale to Duret seems to have sharply cut the number of sales that he made in 1873. Quite possibly, Monet and Durand-Ruel were setting these early 1873 prices in concert, leaving the painter free to sell his own paintings, but on the agreed condition that he respect the dealer's price scale. Such an understanding would have made standard common business sense for both men. And such hypothetical cooperation could have led up to December 9, 1873, when Monet and Durand-Ruel did significant business with one another directly for the last time until 1881. On December 9, 1873, the dealer obtained only nine paintings for 7000 francs, that is, at an average wholesale cost of just under 800 francs each, considerably inflated from the 400-500 francs each cost a few months before, and the 300 francs each cost a few months before that.

1874

Speculating that the dealer and the artist reached an impasse in their business relationship in December 1873 may explain Monet's activities leading up to the first Impressionist exhibition in April 1874. For one thing, the small number of works that Monet submitted to this exhibition might suggest that he had little available to show. After all, Durand-Ruel, who did not lend anything to this independent exhibition, by now had near total control over Monet's exhibitable works.[13] As if to compensate for such a possible predicament, Monet quickly arranged to paint two views from the window of the chosen exhibition space overlooking the Boulevard des Capucines near the Paris Opera House. He included one of these in the Impressionist exhibition.

Meanwhile, on January 13, 1874, Durand-Ruel's client Hoschedé held an auction in Paris of eighty-four works in his collection. Since thirteen of these were recently acquired works by Monet and other Impressionists, the collector was acting like a speculator trying to take a quick profit from the purported inflation of art prices. Durand-Ruel's supervisory role at the auction somewhat precluded the possibility of his bidding, at least openly. Had he been ethically free to bid, however, he would have faced a business dilemma. By showing an active interest in the works, he just might drive the prices up and thus protect the paper value of his inventory of works by Monet. But then Monet himself would be induced to maintain or raise his prices to the dealer in any subsequent transaction. Durand-Ruel opted to wait and see.

The three Monet works in the January 1874 Hoschedé auction sold for only 400, 405, and 550 francs, less than what the painter had charged Durand-Ruel for his paintings just a month before, and presumably much less than what the dealer then might have expected to sell them for. Considering the sequence of events (Monet's decision in December 1873 to raise his prices, then to prepare for the first Impressionist exhibition without the dealer's involvement, followed by the unusually quick buy-sell strategy on the part of Hoschedé), it comes as a surprise that Durand-Ruel, acting on behalf of Hoschedé, then purchased Monet's now famous *Impression, Sunrise*, perhaps the most controversial work on view at the Impressionists' independent exhibition that spring, for 800 francs. Ironically, it would be just this stenographic sort of painting style that got Monet into trouble four or five years later when supporters expressed little interest in the Vétheuil paintings that to them seemed slipshod (an early example was *Bras de la Seine près de Vétheuil*, fig. 3).

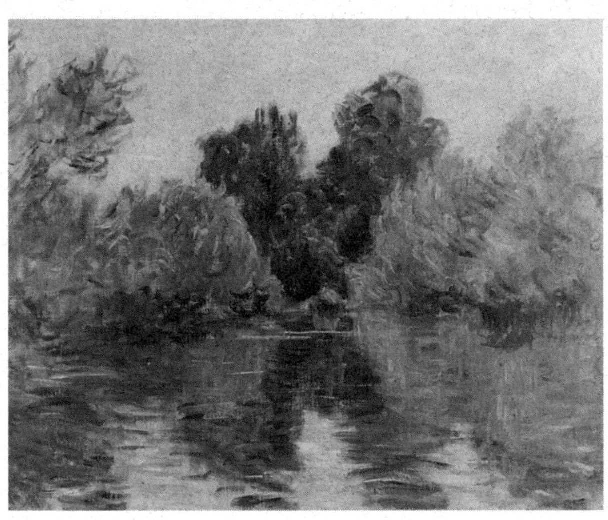

Fig. 3
Claude Monet
Bras de la Seine près de Vétheuil
(Arm of the Seine near Vétheuil)
1878
Oil on canvas
W. 486
Musée des Beaux-Arts, Tours

Although Durand-Ruel implied in his memoirs that he encouraged his clients for Impressionist paintings to do business directly with the artists, it was evidently Manet, not the dealer, who brought opera singer and modern art collector Faure to Monet in June 1874, resulting in a 4000-franc transaction featuring two large early seascapes. But by the end of 1874, as Monet continued selling to Faure, his only major buyer that year, the price per painting returned to 300 francs, the 1872 price level for Durand-Ruel's purchases. What, if any, business relationship existed between Faure and Durand-Ruel is unknown. Unfortunately no photographs or written documents record the appearance of Faure's home, where he presumably hung the scores of works he bought from Monet, Manet, and others. It must have been quite a sight already by the mid-1870s. Eventually Faure owned some fifty Monet works. In any case, by the end of 1874, presumably to cut his expenses now that his income was decreasing from its 1873 high, Monet gave up his Paris studio.[14]

1875-1876

1875 got worse. Instead of an independent group exhibition early that spring, Monet, Morisot, Renoir, and Sisley held their own auction in Paris. Durand-Ruel, acting as supervisor, nevertheless bid on many lots (on behalf of the artists), to prevent their selling for less than minimum prices. The few works that did sell brought low prices. Oddly, neither Faure nor Hoschedé took advantage of the opportunity to acquire Impressionist works at this bargain price level. After the sale, Durand-Ruel paid Monet

200 francs for a seascape that had failed to find a seriously interested bidder. Should this single purchase be understood historically as a sign of Durand-Ruel's support, no matter how small, for Monet? Or, should it be understood as a unique episode of surrender in Monet's seeming attempt to assert control over the market for his own art?

Although Durand-Ruel did rent his exhibition space to the Impressionists for their 1876 group exhibition, at which Monet exhibited many works that had already been collected by Faure, the dealer's space was rented out and thus unavailable in 1877.[15] Meanwhile, many letters written by Monet to fellow artists and collectors provide a vivid sense of his more and more desperate need for money, especially after mid-1876. Curiously, as if Monet realized how pointless it might be to ask Durand-Ruel for any small handout, there is virtually no surviving correspondence between Durand-Ruel and the painter until 1881. This possibly accidental lack of documentation simply adds to the impression that the relationship between the men was strained during these years.

If Durand-Ruel oddly disappears from the Monet picture, however, the figure of Hoschedé grows slightly more distinct in 1876. On April 14, 1876, just before the end of the second Impressionist exhibition on display in Durand-Ruel's space, Hoschedé auctioned more works from his collection in Paris. Since the sale included four paintings by Monet (among them a large new painting of Camille wearing an opulent Japanese robe, W. 387) apparently not owned by Hoschedé, it seems as if the collector and the painter were in some sort of partnership with respect to this auction.

Camille Monet in Japanese Costume sold at this auction for 2000 francs. But only a week later, as if the sale were staged rather than genuine, Monet needed to borrow 1500 francs from Manet's brother, Gustave. Then, beginning in late April 1876, the newly recruited Impressionist painter Gustave Caillebotte began to advance money to Monet against paintings he would select during the next few years. Writing to Pissarro, evidently in July 1876, Cézanne pointed out that Monet was making money.[16] Yet by July 1876, Monet was writing to the collector de Bellio that he was threatened with eviction from his Argenteuil home. Was Monet crying wolf? Then, in December 1876, he was unable to repay Gustave Manet. Why the poverty? In 1876 Monet was paying 1,400 francs in rent while earning over 12,000 francs from the sale of paintings. How could money have been a problem for him?

Only good economic news came to Monet during the last half of 1876. Caillebotte even agreed to pay the rent on a Paris studio for Monet (something Caillebotte would provide until 1882, around the time, coincidentally, when Monet and Durand-Ruel reestablished their lapsed business relationship). Although the idea of retreating to Vétheuil with the Hoschedé family had not yet occurred to Monet, the fact that he again had a Paris studio set the stage for that eventual turn of events. At the time, a trip between Paris and Vétheuil involved a carriage service from Vétheuil to the train station at Mantes.[17] During 1879-1880 Monet's frantic trips, when the weather allowed travel, to sell paintings and borrow money in Paris would all revolve around the studio paid for by Caillebotte.

When Monet took possession in early 1877, this studio near the Saint-Lazare train station served as headquarters for the dozen historic paintings he made with the same train station as subject. Until then, only Courbet had painted such multiple versions of a single subject (seascapes in his case) to exhibit, back in 1866. Why Monet decided to undertake that particular modern subject is open to debate, but it is worth pointing out that throughout 1876 there was considerable interest in one of his paintings, dated 1875, showing a train in the snow;[18] in a small way this suggests that Monet may have wished to capitalize on a potentially marketable new subject.

Much more important, while Monet had recently begun to make as many as four or five variations on a single subject, the idea of basing twelve paintings on a single theme was a milestone in the history of painting in series. Not until the winter of 1879-1880 would Monet again attempt so many variations on a single pictorial subject as he had devoted to the Saint-Lazare train station. Ironically, the awful 1879-1880 winter weather seems to have forced Monet back to the series work that would lead from the 1877 Saint-Lazare railroad station paintings to the *Débâcle* paintings of 1880 to his wheatstacks, poplars, and so on.

Besides the availablity at no charge of a city studio, where Monet could again show works (not just his own, but those of his colleagues, like Pissarro[19]) to prospective buyers, Monet's financial well-being in late 1876 should have been bolstered by the commission that he supposedly received then to paint four large decorative works for the Hoschedé family's country home at Montgeron, not far from where Caillebotte was living at Yerres.[20] Given the 2000-franc auction price supposedly realized in April 1876 for Monet's new large figure painting, it seems reasonable to guess that the Hoschedé commission would have involved the prospect of at least another 5000 francs of income, probably somewhat more. Financial issues aside, Monet's growing familiarity with the Hoschedé family is assumed to have evolved from his work at Montgeron on these large decorative pictures. Since the integration of the Monet and Hoschedé families at Vétheuil is probably the major contextual issue for the 1879-1880 paintings in the present exhibition, it is worth reviewing current assumptions about Monet's working visits to Montgeron.

In fact, almost nothing is known about those visits, including whether or not Monet's large decorative paintings for the Hoschedés were intended to decorate the Montgeron house or to be placed for sale. Moreover, it is worth noting that in 1876 Caillebotte, Renoir, and Whistler, for example, were all also engaged on large-scale works inconsistent with the premises of portable Impressionist painting executed on the spot. Should so much costly, time-consuming activity on large decorative works by so many artists in 1876 be taken as an indication that there was a perceived market for such art now, one that Monet and Hoschedé hoped to address with these four large works?

Even though there was an artist's studio on the grounds in Montgeron, whether Monet painted the large works there is likewise unknown.[21] The assumption that Monet worked on the large pictures *in situ* dovetails with the assumption that he needed to spend lots of time at Montgeron, in turn making it possible to imagine a clandestine love affair. Given the eventual partnership between Alice Hoschedé and the painter, the fact that she gave birth to a son in August 1877 has suggested to recent scholars that Monet, who might have been alone with her around December 1876, could be the likely father.[22] Plausible or not, however, the assumption that Monet and Alice Hoschedé began an affair in 1876 comes from reasoning backwards in time.

Was Ernest Hoschedé always in Paris on business in late 1876? Did he perhaps have his own adulterous love affair keeping him away from home now and in the years ahead? True enough, Monet's son Jean needed to be home in Argenteuil in order to go to school during the week, so presumably Camille needed to stay there with him while Monet was away on assignment. Yet Camille could have taken occasional week-end trips to Montgeron together with her painter-husband: by train, even with a switch in Paris, the journey from Argenteuil to Montgeron was fairly easy. Also worth consideration are the small-scale preliminary "studies" Monet made for these large decorations. Were they made as trials for his clients to approve, prior to development at full scale? Or were these studies made to allow Monet to paint the large versions of the Hoschedé panels in his Paris studio? If Monet indeed painted the large versions at Montgeron, he would have faced some logistical extra effort to transport them to Paris for public display, yet one or two of the large panels were included in the April 1877 Impressionist exhibition in the capital.

As for the possibility of an affair, it suggests a sort of reckless behavior hardly in keeping with the otherwise more reasonable recorded actions of both Alice Hoschedé and Monet throughout their lives. Unless, unbeknownst to historians, the Monets had already established a frequent and close friendship with the Hoschedés, the concept of an affair would by definition suggest impulsive behavior. For Monet, his part in the alleged love affair would have meant risking a duel with one of his very few potential clients at the time. And if Alice, without knowing the painter very well yet, initiated anything improperly passionate at this time, Monet might well have been disinclined to trust her as his own life partner in later years. Indeed, Alice Hoschedé was a devout Catholic, who would take charge of arranging the final rites for the dying Camille.[23] Monet, on the other hand, has generally been described as a free thinker where religion is concerned.[24] Presumably the antithetical religious attitudes of Monet and Alice Hoschedé would have been a barrier, perhaps not to an affair, but more seriously to common-law marriage. But, then, perhaps Monet was more deeply religious than he has been imagined to be. He certainly included churches in his paintings as much as or more than any other artist, at least starting in Vétheuil in 1878. Could it be that Alice Hoschedé was in fact a catalyst for piety rather than impropriety in Monet's life?

1877

At the beginning of 1877, while Monet was at work based at his Paris studio on his Saint-Lazare train station variations and perhaps also on the large-scale versions of the Montgeron murals, Hoschedé himself went on an art-buying spree, albeit on credit. In January he bought twenty-seven Impressionist works from Durand-Ruel, and then in March he bought seven additional works from Monet, including perhaps four of the Saint-Lazare train station variations. Although these Saint-Lazare acquisitions could be understood as a revolutionary new form of art collecting in series, it seems at least as likely that Hoschedé was buying stock to sell as a dealer. In June and July Hoschedé advanced 750 francs to Monet for another work apparently not yet selected. Then in August 1877 Hoschedé was obliged to declare bankruptcy.[25] What seems so remarkable is the coincidental synchronicity, more or less, between Hoschedé's financial ruin and Monet's own unaccountable money collapse. The fact that the Monet and Hoschedé families reacted to their individual plights by joining forces in 1878, however, suggests the possibility that the two downfalls may have been interrelated. One can only wonder whether the events leading from Monet's break with Durand-Ruel at the end of 1873 until his move to Vétheuil with the Hoschedés nearly five years later might make more sense had there been some sort of business partnership between artist and collector.

The possibility that Hoschedé and Monet had been silent partners in a badly failed art market venture could answer two otherwise inescapable questions, both fundamental to why Monet went to Vétheuil and was stranded there by accident with nothing to paint but his *Débâcles*, changing the course of his art career forever. The questions, of course, are: what *did* happen to all Monet's 1870s earnings, and how did he and his family come to be on close terms with the Hoschedés? Of course, just because such a partnership, never once suggested by Monet's own account books from the period, might help answer these questions hardly proves that there was such a partnership. But it does seem no less unlikely than the assumption that Monet and Alice Hoschedé brought their families together to Vétheuil from unbridled illicit passion for one another.

1878

When in late January the Monets, Camille over seven months pregnant, moved from Argenteuil to Paris, their rent went down from 1400 to 1360 francs. Monet had to borrow 1200 francs from Manet earlier that same month, perhaps to manage the move. Very much aware that Hoschedé's bankruptcy would result in the sale of his large Impressionist collection at auction, the Impressionist painters discussed the possibility of a group show, but these discussions resulted only in internal dissension among them. At issue was whether or not an artist could exhibit works both at the Salon and simultaneously at an exhibition organized by their cooperative, as Renoir wished to do.[26] This seems worth mentioning, if only because when Monet joined Renoir as a Salon exhibitor in 1880, his fortunes would suddenly change, as if the fact that he broke away from the group this way made it possible for him almost immediately to get back on his feet financially, even though his participation at the Salon of 1880 was hardly a success in any direct way.

It seems quite possible that Duret's 1878 pamphlet, *Les Peintres impressionistes*, which placed the artists within the tradition of nineteenth-century French modern art and listed the collectors and critics that gave them support (minus Durand-Ruel and Hoschedé), was designed to head off possible disaster at the forthcoming Hoschedé bankruptcy auction. No matter, the Hoschedé auction was a disaster that all but ruined Pissarro, nine of whose works were dispersed in it.[27] As for Renoir, only three of his works were in the auction, suggesting that his relationship to Hoschedé was far less active than Monet's or Pissarro's. Although prices for the three Renoir works were low, by 1878 he had developed a career as an Impressionist decorative artist and portraitist, whose clients included the Charpentier publishing family that would play such a crucial role in Monet's professional recovery at the beginning of 1880.

Not surprisingly, the Hoschedé bankruptcy auction raises its share of questions about the Monet-Hoschedé relationship. Sixteen works by Monet were in the early

June 1878 auction. But only twelve of these were listed in the sale catalogue. To whom did the other four belong? One of these was bought on behalf of Monet by dealer Georges Petit, who in the 1880s would become a formidable rival to Durand-Ruel in the Impressionist market.[28] It was Petit, not Durand-Ruel this time, who handled Hoschedé's auction. (By the way, at the time he declared bankruptcy, Hoschedé owed 70,000 francs to Petit, but owed only 12,500 francs to Durand-Ruel.[29]) Given Monet's desperate financial straits at the time, it seems curious that the painter would buy back a work already sold to Hoschedé at this bankruptcy auction, even if as little as thirty-eight francs were involved. As likely, Monet himself added these four uncatalogued works to the sale, setting minimum acceptable prices which he had instructed Petit to protect. Works supposedly belonging to Hoschedé, but curiously not in the sale, included all the large decorative panels undertaken at the end of 1876 at Montgeron. Two of the studies for these larger works, however, were included. And only one Saint-Lazare train station was sold, whereas Hoschedé had bought as many as four a year before. Had these "missing" works been sold by Hoschedé prior to bankruptcy? It is worth mentioning that Monet, in an undated letter to Duret, provided prices for works by Courbet and Morisot that belonged to Hoschedé. Were these prices provided because Hoschedé wished to sell them on the side, before the auction? Or does Monet's letter to Duret indicate that Hoschedé was prepared to act as a dealer for works in his own collection?[30] After the June 1878 auction Hoschedé continued to buy and sell works. Already in July 1878 he bought a new painting by Monet, which he immediately sold to the musician Chabrier (W. 470). As early as August 1878 the two families got together in Vétheuil.

Surviving correspondence indicates that Hoschedé handled sales of new Monet paintings in Paris while the artist painted the landscape at Vétheuil, making still lifes when bad weather made outdoor work impossible.[31] If one could only find a word for Ernest Hoschedé's relationship with Monet ("patron," "friend," "partner," "agent"), the history of Impressionism would read far more clearly than it so far has.

1879

Monet's greatest achievement during 1879 was to overcome near total demoralization, with the help of friends, Alice Hoschedé most of all. Although he was desperate for sales, he would not have taken part in the Impressionist group exhibition that year except for the efforts of Caillebotte, who arranged to gather together a fair number of works from lenders and even prompted Monet to send some new ones, two of them in need of repairs, since the depressed Monet had slashed at them in dissatisfaction.

Monet never went to see the exhibition, which ran from April 10 until May 11.[32] Was he too ashamed about facing gossips wagging their tongues over his misery and his living arrangement with Alice Hoschedé out in the country? Having concluded that he should now unburden the Hoschedés of his own family's troubles, Monet wrote in May 1879 from Vétheuil to Ernest in Paris, asking for an account of what he still owed in terms of shared household expenses.[33]

More likely what kept him away from Paris in the spring of 1879 was his reluctance to take sides in the politics dividing the other Impressionists. Instead of participating in the 1879 Impressionist group show, Monet's friends Cézanne, Renoir, and Sisley all opted to send works to the Salon's admissions jury. In June 1879, Renoir had a one-artist exhibition in a brand new little gallery sponsored by a lifestyle periodical, *La Vie Moderne*, published since April 1879 by his clients the Charpentiers. It would be at this gallery that Monet first exhibited his *Débâcle* paintings in the spring of 1880, just months after he did in the end decide to take sides with the lapsed Impressionists sending works to the Salon. While Camille Monet was dying in Vétheuil, her old friend Renoir was summering on the Normandy coast not far from where she and Monet had lived a decade before. It was Renoir's good luck not to have had much to do with the Hoschedés. In steady demand as a portrait painter, with such influential clients as the Charpentiers, by 1879 he had commissions to decorate country homes and opportunities to paint the sort of coastscape that would obsess Monet by the end of 1880. As for Ernest Hoschedé, by mid-November 1879, two months after Camille's burial, Monet wrote to him from Vétheuil, urging him to visit home and bring along badly needed money to meet household expenses. Then the bad weather took over.

Snow and bitter cold forced Monet indoors to paint still lifes in the second half of November. He was lucky, too, since these sold better in the following months than his landscapes. Petit would pay 500 francs for one in December 1879 and another 500 francs for a second, this of dead pheasants, in February 1880. Monet had not received as much for any of his works since 1876. Financially speaking, landscape painter Monet was saved by his work in still life.

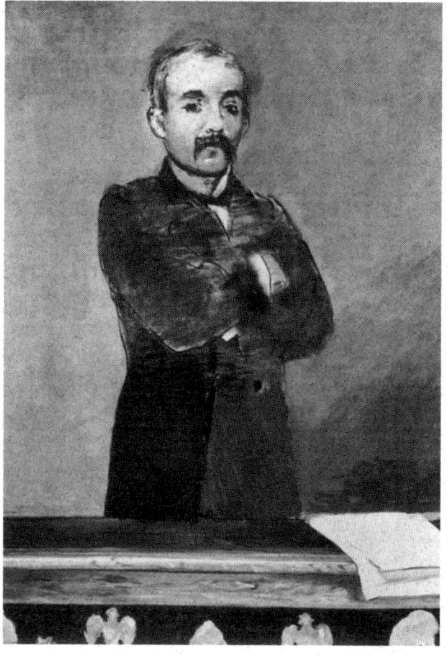

Fig. 4
Édouard Manet
Portrait de Georges Clemenceau
(Portrait of Georges Clemenceau)
1879-1880
Oil on canvas
Kimbell Art Museum, Forth Worth, Texas

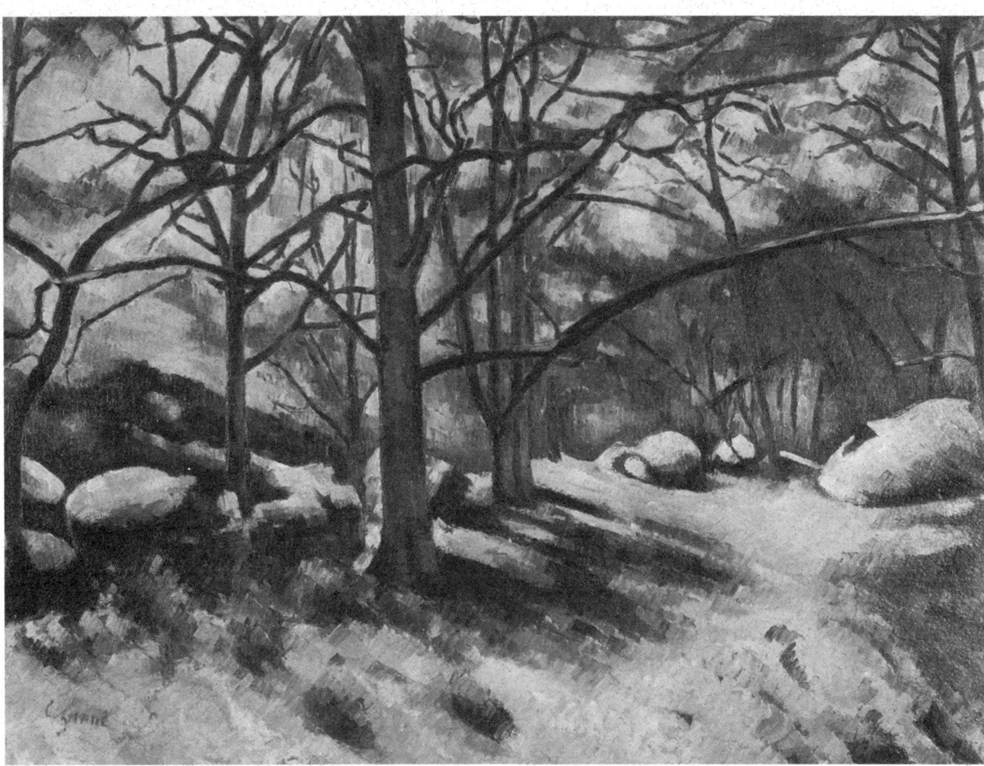

Fig. 5
Paul Cézanne
Neige fondante à Fontainebleau
(Melting Snow, Fontainebleau)
Ca. 1879-1880
Oil on canvas
The Museum of Modern Art, New York. Gift of André Meyer

In December 1879 Monet's future best friend Georges Clemenceau was evidently posing for his portrait at Manet's Paris studio (fig. 4).[34] Meanwhile Zola cancelled appointments in Paris, snowbound at his country house in Medan while at work on his sensationalist novel *Nana*. The mails must have been slowed down considerably, but Zola corresponded with Flaubert, who was vainly trying to finish *Bouvard and Pécuchet*. Like his childhood friend Zola, Cézanne, who was living near Fontainebleau Forest in Melun, was short on coal.[35] Possibly this snowy winter was when Cézanne, working from a photograph rather than venturing out-of-doors, painted the forest snowscape (fig. 5) that Monet, when he became rich again, bought for a record-setting auction price in 1899. It is not known whether or not Cézanne had submitted this topical snowscape to the Salon of 1880, when poverty-stricken Monet likewise submitted the same sort of subject. If submitted, Cézanne's winterscape, like Monet's, was refused by the admissions jury. But the 1879-1880 winter paintings executed by Gauguin (fig. 6) and Guillaumin were put on public view in April 1880 at the fifth Impressionist exhibition, where the works by Cézanne, Sisley (fig. 7), and Monet would have been welcome.

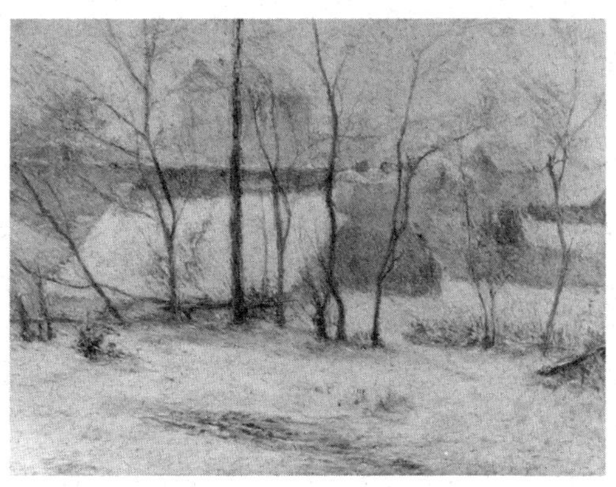

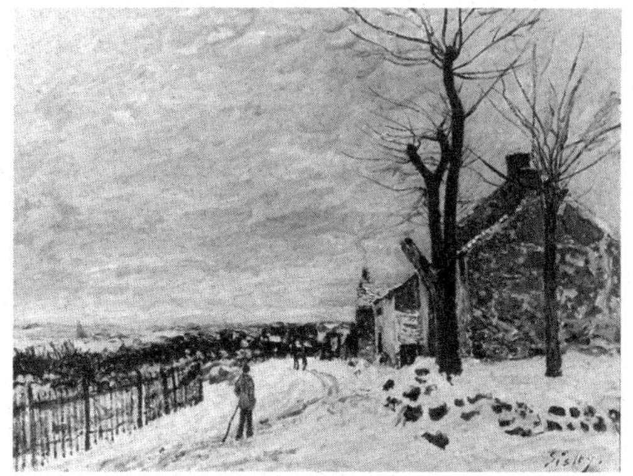

Fig. 6 (left)
Paul Gauguin
Jardin dans la neige
(Garden in the Snow)
1879
Oil on canvas
Fine Arts Museum, Budapest

Fig. 7 (right)
Alfred Sisley
Temps de neige à Veneux-Nadon
(Snowy Weather at Veneux-Nadon)
Ca. 1880
Oil on canvas
Musée d'Orsay, Paris

1880

When the weather warmed and the frozen Seine thawed in early January the Monets and Hoschedés (minus Ernest, who was unable to reach Vétheuil, even for a family Christmas), witnessed the landscape as it had never appeared before. With awesome, near glacial power, the river current carried noisy, menacing blocks of ice and debris downstream. Monet lost no time, and by January 8, 1880 had begun work on a group of around twenty closely related paintings. Even synchronizing the speed of his eye to observe with the speed of his hand to record, in the classic sketchy Impressionist manner he had helped to invent during the previous fifteen years, Monet could never have made so many variations in the available time before the awesome natural episode disappeared from view. While he worked, either outdoors or inside, he surely remembered his own efforts in the mid-1860s (fig. 8) to rival Courbet's snowscapes (fig. 9). For example, in the winter of 1867-1868 he had even made two icy riverscapes (W. 105-106). But those works, painted at Bougival, were anecdotal, lacking all the majesty of his empty, houseless, peopleless *Débâcle* paintings.[36]

Word of Monet's excitement about his dramatic new work spread fast, possibly thanks to Hoschedé in Paris. The hateful article carried in *Le Gaulois* on January 24 was well enough informed to announce that Monet would be submitting something to the Salon in a few weeks. Monet had indeed decided to submit two large-scale paintings, a wintry *Débâcle* scene based on portable-sized versions he had made in early January, and a summery scene on the Seine looking toward the village of Lavacourt.

This latter composition showed one of the first subjects that Monet had opted to paint in Vétheuil, perhaps already in late 1878. By the end of 1879 he had already sold two or three of the five versions he painted of this same composition showing tree-covered little islands flooded by the calm sunlit river and, on its far side, the town of

Lavacourt (W. 475, W. 539, and W. 541).[37] While the Salon admissions jury refused to accept the grand *Débâcle* painting, it accepted the less bleak view of Lavacourt.

Waiting for the Salon to open, contemporary art lovers in Paris that April could have visited the fifth Impressionist exhibition, or they could have visited the gallery associated with *La Vie Moderne* to see an exhibition of new works by Manet. Hoschedé had a few recent Monet paintings to show possible buyers at the offices of the deluxe periodical he was founding, *L'Art et la Mode*, the first issue of which would appear in August 1880. Aside from getting his new business off the ground that April, which so preoccupied him that he neglected to visit his family at Easter, Hoschedé was working in tandem with Duret on arrangements for a Monet exhibition at the gallery of *La Vie Moderne*.[38] Was he being cuckolded by the artist he was helping?

Nothing is known about how and exactly when this badly needed solo exhibition opportunity came Monet's way. The available documentation in letters suggests that after the first week in April, when the jury decisions were released, Monet's friends must have realized that the rejection of the *Débâcle* painting had been a hard blow. One or more of them, Manet or Renoir presumably, very quickly persuaded the gallery manager of *La Vie Moderne* to let Monet have a show there, in which the refused *Débâcle* painting (and others of its ilk, such as *Le Givre*, fig. 10) could be celebrated. Duret rushed to write a catalogue essay in time for the June 6 opening, while Manet provided a thumbnail sketch of Monet to illustrate this little publication marking the first one-artist exhibition in Monet's career, an exhibition coming just when his life was at its darkest hour. *La Vie Moderne* even sent a writer to Vétheuil to interview

Fig. 8 (left)
Claude Monet
Environs de Honfleùr, neige
(The Environs of Honfleur, Snow)
1867
W. 79
Oil on canvas
Musée du Louvre, Paris

Fig. 9 (right)
Gustave Courbet
L'Hiver (Winter)
1872-1873
Oil on canvas
Felton Bequest, 1922
National Gallery of Victoria, Melbourne, Australia

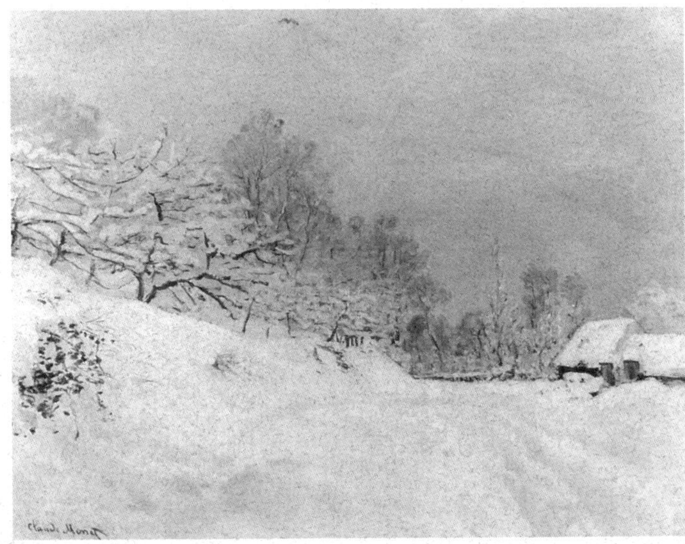

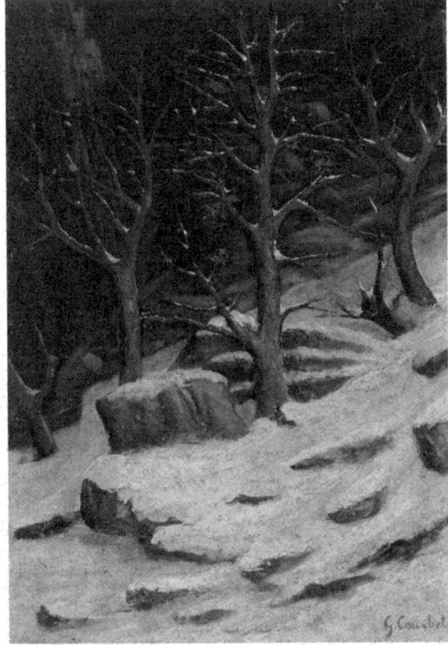

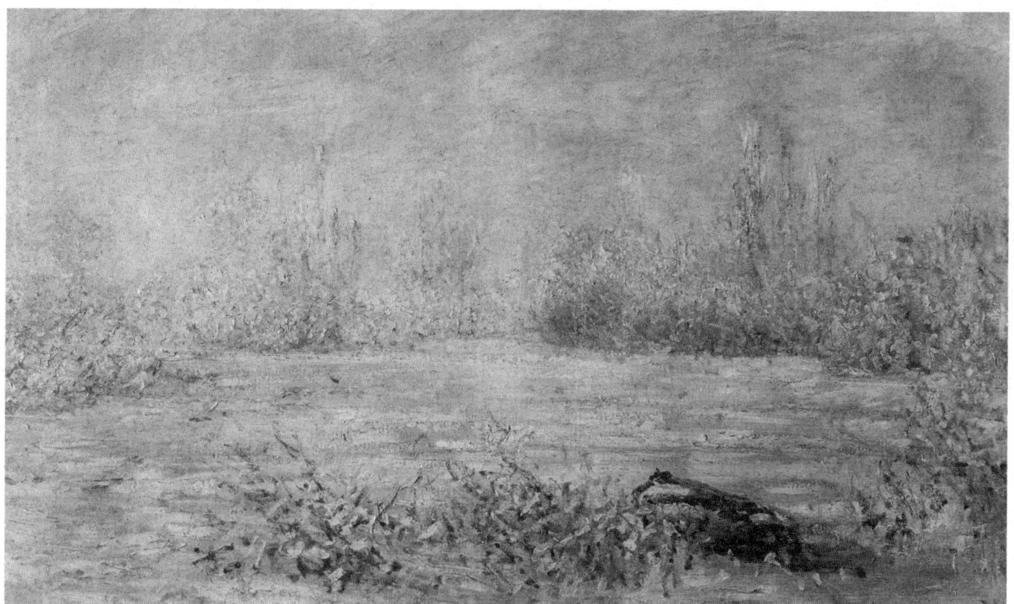

Monet for a feature article that appeared in the June 12 issue. Best of all, Monet was able to sell the large *Débâcle* painting to Madame Charpentier for 1500 francs, a price unheard-of for Monet since before Hoschedé became a factor in his life way back in 1873.

Evidently word of Monet's success quickly reached an old creditor who now took his cut of the sales proceeds for the Charpentiers' *Débâcle*.[39] It hardly mattered! Monet's career was off and running again, even more quickly than it had gone off track in the mid-1870s. At the end of the summer, Monet took a "vacation" (where Monet was concerned the term should always be "working vacation") to visit his older brother on the Normandy coast. There he tried a few coastscapes in emulation of those Renoir had been painting since the year before. By December 1880 Monet even considered a trip to London to paint some views of the city he had not seen for a decade. As it turned out, he was unable to start work on those London views for another twenty years. At the end of 1880, Monet went to Paris to attend the funeral on December 12 of Ernest Hoschedé's mother.[40] Could he possibly have shown his face on that occasion if he were then stealing the mother of Hoschedé's children?

In February 1881, as if nothing had ever intervened in their close business relationship, Durand-Ruel bought fifteen new paintings from Monet, at his original 1872 benchmark price of 300 francs. Whoever got them to bury the hatchet, presuming there was one to bury, Monet and Durand-Ruel now began the famous business

Fig. 10
Claude Monet
Le Givre (Frost)
1880
Oil on canvas
W. 555
Musée d'Orsay, Paris

relationship that would bring Impressionism to the world and make the painter a rich man. Judging from Monet's account records, which for quite a stretch after this time show no sales to other clients, they had agreed that Durand-Ruel would have exclusive rights to obtain Monet's new works from then on. And in return Monet could count on the money he needed to paint and live. For his part, Durand-Ruel may still have wanted other subtler forms of revenge, such as commissioning from Monet, by 1882 at the latest, a suite of decorative still-life paintings to adorn the panels of the doors for the grand sitting room where the dealer would show off his large Renoir paintings.

Monet immediately began to settle a few old financial debts,[41] and by May 1881 at the latest he made plans to move away from Vétheuil. Remarkably enough, when Monet and his sons did relocate to Poissy in December of 1881, Alice Hoschedé and her six children accompanied them. Surely now she and the painter had a spousal relationship, forged by overcoming terrible challenges together. Moreover the economic panic that apparently led Monet in early 1877 to paint so many Saint-Lazare train station variations and then again in early 1880 to revisit the risky market strategy by making so many *Débâcles*, eventually showed him the way to overcome the sort of sketchiness that had been so problematic for him with respect to collectors and critics in the horrible late 1870s.

In early 1880 at Vétheuil, bad weather prevented Monet from finding more than one or two related motifs. As he worked away from home in 1882 in Normandy, where motifs were plentiful, however, he seemed to realize how, logistically, if he could arrange to cart several canvases to one particlar work site, along with all his other needed supplies, he then could paint progressively on several works in series on a single day, starting or resuming work on any one of them as specific light conditions returned, with a certain amount of predictability, from one day to the next. When the light changed, he set his painting in process aside to await another session at the same site. Meanwhile, without losing time on any given day by going from one site to another, he could choose another variation of the same composition to work up, and so on. With cooperation from the weather, such a working method in theory allowed Monet to give each individual work more attention than ever. Using the series concept this way, he could maintain his strict standards of realist transcription. And, with multiple sessions at any one given motif, his aggregate efforts would result in sufficient finish to satisfy everyone, himself included.

Moreover, in his new relationship with Alice Hoschedé, the entire structure of Monet's social life was transformed. Some old friends among the original Impressionists who had felt comfortable visiting Monet when Camille was alive would play reduced roles in his new life. But a whole new network of colleagues took shape, many with Giverny connections. With all this in mind, it is difficult not to judge the debacle of January 1880 as the turning point in Monet's entire career. Upon consideration, three unexpected events played the major roles in this crucial episode: the worst winter weather in memory; the ugly hatred of some enemy with influence at a Paris newspaper; and finally a guardian angel who stepped forward during the first week in April and made possible the exhibition at *La Vie Moderne*. Humbling though it is to admit, historians have no better explanation for the surprising human interventions than meteorologists have for the weird weather.

YEARS LATER

The winter after Monet and Alice Hoschedé married in 1892, the painter did a few snowscape variations showing blocks of ice on the Seine near Giverny. These amount to a sort of revisitation of the 1880 *Débâcle* paintings, now done without any of the paint-or-else compulsion at issue when times were very bad. In February 1895 the fifty-five-year-old Monet sought out the challenge of painting in the arctic cold, visiting Oslo, Norway, where one of his stepsons was living. Jacques Hoschedé helped transport his stepfather to viewpoints where he painted in bearskins. Six years after that, while workers enlarged his water garden at Giverny, Monet rented a house in Lavacourt for his family to escape from the commotion. There he painted fifteen square-format views of Vétheuil from the balcony of the house. The memories invested in the series paintings Monet made that summer can scarcely be guessed at. In January 1909, while Alice was very sick (she died two years later), Monet wrote to a friend that he badly wished he could paint the snow-covered landscape. But although at sixty-eight years of age the enduringly successful Monet might well be described as a "lion in winter," by now he no longer felt strong enough to paint outdoors in bad weather.

Notes

1 Joel Isaacson, *Observation and Reflection, Claude Monet* (Oxford, 1978), 23.

2 It is worth pondering the relationship, if any, between Alfred Meyer, according to Rewald manager and president of an artists' group (L'Union) to which Cézanne and Pissarro belonged in 1875, and Arthur Meyer, the director of *Le Gaulois*: about the former, Cézanne wrote Pissarro on July 2, 1876, "But Meyer must be very eager to damage Monet." See Paul Cézanne, *Letters*, ed. John Rewald (New York, 4th and revised ed., 1976), 147; and Daniel Wildenstein, *Claude Monet: Biographie et catalogue raisonné*, vol. 1 (Lausanne, 1974), 107-108.

3 According to the recollections of Alice and Ernest Hoschedé's daughter, Blanche, who eventually married Monet's eldest son, the families' joint trip to Vétheuil in the late summer of 1878 was at first intended as a vacation, not as a long-term house-sharing plan. See Jean-Pierre Hoschedé, *Claude Monet, ce mal connu* (Geneva, 1960), 1:158. Otherwise, there is scarcely any information about the genesis of the merger of the families; see Wildenstein 1974, 1:92.

4 Wildenstein 1974, 1:83.

5 *Ibid.*, 1:80 and 431 (letter 99). Monet's undated letter to de Bellio from Argenteuil explains that Camille is suffering from an ulcerated uterus and that the local doctor recommended surgery. Whether she conceived Michel before or after this diagnosis is uncertain.

6 Emile Zola, *L'Oeuvre*, Paris, 1886, chapters 9-10. See Robert J. Niess, *Zola, Cézanne, and Manet, A Study of* L'Oeuvre (Ann Arbor, 1968), 174.

7 During 1872 Durand-Ruel also bought other Monet works from collectors and dealers to whom Monet had previously sold them, for example W. 84 and W. 210.

8 See Wildenstein 1974, 1:63; and Paul Tucker, *Claude Monet, Life and Art* (New Haven and London, 1995), 57.

9 Later, in 1888, Monet withheld his consent for the exhibition with works by him at a Durand-Ruel gallery for which an admission fee was charged; see Wildenstein, *Claude Monet: Biographie et catalogue raisonné*, vol. 3 (Lausanne, 1979), 9.

10 For a survey of artists' efforts during the 1860s and 1870s to stage their own independent group exhibitions, see Paul Tucker, "The First Impressionist Exhibition in Context," in *The New Painting, Impression 1874-1886*, (San Francisco, 1986), 94-96.

11 Paul Durand-Ruel, "Mémoires" in *Les Archives de l'Impressionisme*, ed. Lionello Venturi (Paris and New York, 1939), 2:197-199.

12 As Duret explained in a letter to Pissarro, "It was Manet himself who, discussing the price of this painting with me, talked to me of this 1200 francs price, which fully confirms the fact of the reduction that was made for me from 1500 and 1200 to 1200 and 1000, which reduction alone allowed me to buy the painting." See Wildenstein 1974, 1:445 (*pièce justificative* 28 *bis*).

13 The sudden suspension of business between Monet and Durand-Ruel is paralleled by a rupture between the dealer and Degas. Degas' purchase of a painting by Pissarro from Durand-Ruel on December 16, 1873, was the last direct transaction between them until late 1880. In March 1874, just weeks before the first Impressionist exhibition opened, Degas arranged for Faure to buy all the works of his in Durand-Ruel's possession. See Michael Pantazzi, "Chronology II: 1873-1881" in *Degas* (New York and Ottawa, 1988), 212 and 221. As for Renoir, he continued to sell to Durand-Ruel occasionally in the mid-1870s and even painted the portrait of the dealer's daughter, Jeanne (today at the Barnes Foundation, Merion, Pennsylvania).

14 Wildenstein 1974, 1:57.

15 Marie Berhaut, *Caillebotte, sa vie et son oeuvre* (Paris, 1978), 243 (letter 3).

16 Cézanne, *Letters*, 1976,146-147.

17 Wildenstein 1974, 1:92.

18 *Ibid.*, 1:429-430 and 445 (letters 80, 91, and *pièce justificative* 29).

19 Camille Pissarro, *Correspondance*, ed. Janine Bailly-Herzberg (Paris, 1980), 1:117 (letter 61).

20 Wildenstein 1974, 1:82-83; and Hélène Adhémar, "Ernest Hoschedé," in *Aspects of Monet*, eds. John Rewald and Frances Weitzenhoffer (New York, 1984), 52-71. Oddly enough, the complete absence of documentation gives no idea of what relationship, if any, may have existed between Hoschedé and Caillebotte, Monet's two most important patrons in the late 1870s.

21 Wildenstein 1974, 1:82.

22 *Ibid.*, 1:83.

23 *Ibid.*, 1:98.

24 Wildenstein, *Claude Monet, Biographie et catalogue raisonné*, vol. 4 (Lausanne, 1985), 142.

25 Wildenstein 1974, 1:91-92; and Adhémar 1984, 62-66.

26 Ronald Pickvance, "Contemporary Popularity and Posthumous Neglect" in *The New Painting*, 1986, 243-246.

27 Pissarro 1974, 1:13 (letter 57).

28 Merete Bodelson, "Early Impressionist Sales 1874-94 in the light of some unpublished 'procès-verbaux'," *The Burlington Magazine* CX, no. 783 (June 1968): 339-340; and Wildenstein 1974, 1:434 (letter 135).

29 Wildenstein 1974, 1:91.

30 *Ibid.*, 1:92 and 434 (letter 134).

31 *Ibid.*, 1:439 and 446 (letter 178 and *pièces justificatives* 39, 42, and 47); and Wildenstein, *Claude Monet: Biographie et catalogue raisonné*, vol. 5 (Lausanne, 1991), 189 and 216 (letters 2697, 2702, and 3091).

32 Wildenstein 1974, 1:95-96; and Pickvance 1986, 243-265.

33 Wildenstein 1974, 1:437 (letter 158).

34 Françoise Cachin and Charles S. Moffett, *Manet 1832-1883*, (New York,1983), 443.

35 Emile Zola, *Correspondance*, ed. B.H. Bakker (Montréal and Paris, 1982), 3:414 ff; and Cézanne, *Letters*, 1976, 184.

36 Wildenstein 1974, 1:106-107; and Isaacson 1978, 196-197.

37 What seems to be a typograpical error in Wildenstein 1991, 5:32, has W. 475 possibly sold in February 1878, before Monet could have painted it. Although Monet's Salon version of this composition (plate 7) received little attention when first shown, this same painting would be one of the first that Durand-Ruel would purchase when he resumed business with Monet in February 1881.

38 Wildenstein 1974, 1:116, 439-441 (letters 179, 191 and 197); and Adhémar 1984, 66-67.

39 *Ibid.*, 1:440-441 (letters 186. 192 and 198).

40 *Ibid.*, 1:116.

41 Wildenstein 1991, 5:189 and 216 (letters 2704 and 3092).

Carole McNamara

MONET'S VÉTHEUIL PAINTINGS: SITE, SUBJECT, AND *DÉBÂCLES*

Claude Monet's paintings of Argenteuil, with their promenades and sailboats, are among the first paintings to come to mind when we think of Impressionism. Similarly, the large canvases of his water-lily garden, executed in the final decades of his life at Giverny, seem to connect the painting of the nineteenth and twentieth centuries. However, less well-known are the works that Monet produced in the brief period that lies between the years at Argenteuil and those at Giverny. The residency that began, according to Blanche Hoschedé, as a summer rental together with the family of his friend, Ernest Hoschedé,[1] evolved into a three-year stay, from which his family and his art emerged renewed and redirected. The paintings dating from his stay at Vétheuil were produced under tremendous personal, financial, and artistic hardships. These three years were to prove pivotal in Monet's life and career, and we can chart the change in his artistic fortunes through the shifts in his subject matter, the manner in which he portrayed his new home, and the impressive series of paintings that resulted from the severe cold and flood during the winter of 1879-1880.

By the time that Monet had settled along the Seine at his new home in Vétheuil he had long been recognized as a leader of the Impressionists. He was hailed by Émile Zola and other critics as an artist who, like Édouard Manet, Edgar Degas, and Pierre-Auguste Renoir, was dedicated to the depiction of contemporary life. The paintings he produced during his seven-year stay at Argenteuil reflected the interests and mores of modern French society.[2] Among the subjects portrayed at Argenteuil were scenes of yachting, promenades along the river bank, and residential gardens; these views of Argenteuil were balanced with views of Paris from the same period, as Monet took the train to his studio near the Gare Saint-Lazare and participated in the Impressionist group exhibitions between 1874 and 1882. The paintings of Paris include views along the boulevards and parks, flag-draped streets, and, finally, the group of paintings that he executed under the steamy shed at the railroad station, the Gare Saint-Lazare. We can conclude that the focus of Monet's paintings prior to his move to Vétheuil was largely devoted to contemporary figures within settings that were primarily urban and suburban; in these works his interests were akin to Baudelaire's *flâneur*, observing and recording modern Parisian life. Even views of the countryside around Argenteuil included figures, usually his wife Camille (née Doncieux), and young son Jean. During the Argenteuil years the Impressionists were united in the desire to capture modernity, and they even worked with one another, depicting each other at work painting. A number of other painters in the group, including Manet and Renoir, visited Monet while he was living at Argenteuil, attesting to the bonds of this confraternity of painters who had begun to show together in Paris and who had all suffered repeated rejection by the juries of the official Salon.

Increasing difficulties in Monet's ability to sell his pictures through the Paris-based dealer Paul Durand-Ruel resulted in his family's departure from Argenteuil to Paris late in the summer of 1878, leaving behind a number of creditors.[3] In addition to contending with straitened family finances, Monet felt that Argenteuil was becoming too built up and sought a new location farther from the encroaching sprawl of Paris.[4]

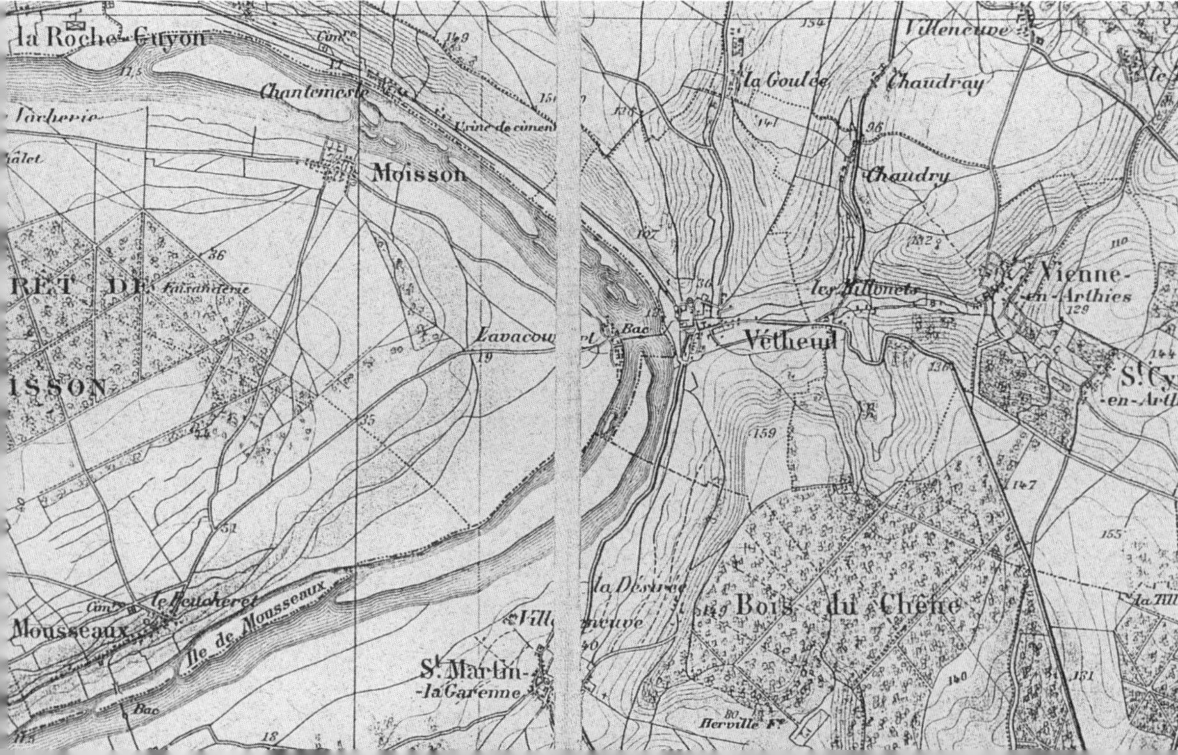

Fig. 1
A map of Vétheuil from 1900, detail
Cartothèque, Institut Géographique National, Paris

He settled in August of that year at Vétheuil, a small farming community downriver from Argenteuil, not far from his final home along a tributary of the Seine at Giverny.

Notable in guidebooks for its small Gothic church dedicated to the Virgin, the town of Vétheuil (fig. 1) must have seemed a sleepy hamlet compared to Argenteuil. At Vétheuil the Seine is divided in two by a series of islands which separate Vétheuil from the town on the opposite bank, Lavacourt. The main shipping channel for barge traffic along the river was on the Lavacourt side, and Monet settled into a house on the southern edge of Vétheuil, later renting a house with property extending to the river's edge, where he could moor his studio boat. Vétheuil was quite removed from the suburban activity embodied by Argenteuil, Poissy, and other towns within easy reach of Parisians. The nearest train access was at the town of Mantes-la-Jolie, some twelve kilometers away.[5] There were no bridges across the Seine at Vétheuil, and commerce between it and Lavacourt was carried on by means of a ferry that ran between the two towns.[6]

With his arrival in Vétheuil, there began a gradual shift in Monet's choice of subject matter. His paintings of the Gare Saint-Lazare in 1877, the Parc Monceau, and the flag-draped festivities along the Rue Saint-Denis and Rue Montorgueil in 1878—all painted prior to his move to Vétheuil—were the last canvases he would paint of Paris. Although he continued to travel frequently to Paris in order to exhibit his works and meet with dealers and prospective clients, the capital, with its cafés and boulevards, was never to appear again in his paintings. Even among his landscape paintings there was a subtle adjustment in emphasis. No longer did they show suburban promenades as they had at Argenteuil; the landscapes become more rural, with the human presence reduced and occasionally totally removed as Monet looked back to earlier Barbizon painting in which the viewer is alone in the rural landscape. This neo-Romantic direction would manifest itself again in many of Monet's canvases once he settled in Giverny.[7]

Monet's early paintings of Vétheuil include scenes of Lavacourt, the town across the river (W. 475-476, W. 495-500), and of the approaches to Vétheuil from the main highway and from La Roche-Guyon to the northwest (W. 502, W. 508-510). He also depicted during this first year a number of views of the church, seen both from the near shore of the Seine and from across the river at Lavacourt. Several of these sites would be revisited in the paintings of the frozen Seine during the particularly harsh winter of 1879-1880.

In many of his early views of Vétheuil, Monet depicted certain aspects and features of the village, and disregarded others. A lithograph by Adolphe Maugendre

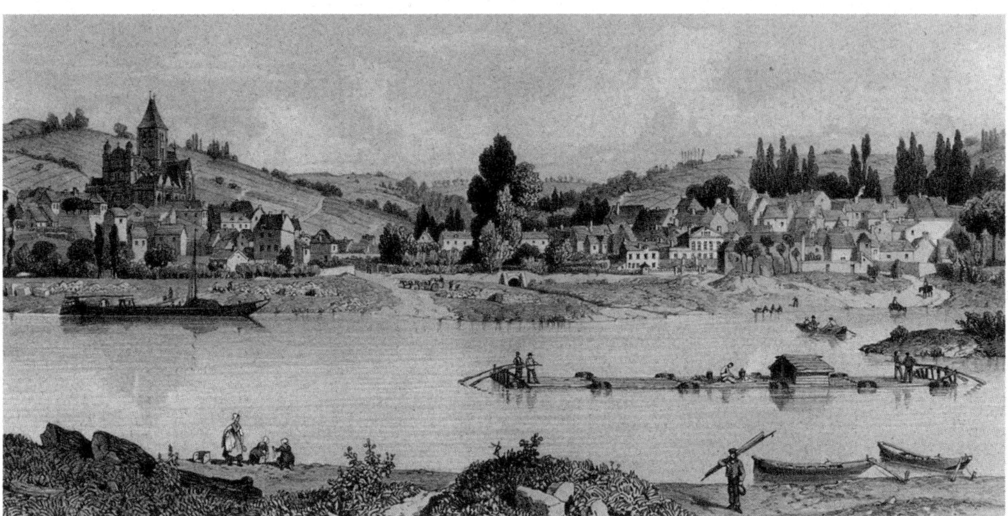

Fig. 2
Adolphe Maugendre
Vétheuil, Vue générale, prise de Lavacourt
(General View of Vétheuil from Lavacourt)
1853
Département des estampes et de la photographie, Bibliothèque nationale de France, Paris

(1809-1895) drawn in 1853, for example, shows the town as seen from Lavacourt on the opposite bank (fig. 2). Full of quotidian detail, the print portrays Vétheuil as tidy and prosperous; the church of Notre-Dame is visible at the left with the town extending upstream in the direction of Mantes-la-Jolie to the right. The Seine and its banks are bustling with activity. Washerwomen and boats can be seen on the Lavacourt side; ships, fishermen, and the barges that run downriver animate the surface of the water in the middleground; workmen loading cargo and washerwomen occupy the far bank. Implicit in this view of Vétheuil is its relationship to the river. Monet's paintings of Vétheuil, seen from roughly the same vantage point, will include references to structures and the town's physical relationship to the river, but will exclude much of the lively, anecdotal detail represented in the Maugendre lithograph by the figures going about their daily tasks.

The Seine at this time was still a major commercial thoroughfare in France, even after the rebuilding of the railway system damaged during the Franco-Prussian War of 1870-1871. Barges plied the waters of the Seine, bringing goods to Paris from ports along the Normandy coast such as Le Havre, making the Seine an important means of furnishing Paris with luxuries and necessities for its ever-increasing population. Islands dot the river where it forms an ox-bow at Vétheuil; this string of islands, the Île de Moisson and Île Saint-Martin among them, effectively created a mid-river screen that separated Vétheuil from the shipping along the river.[8] Monet, in settling at this bend of the river, avoided the commercial thoroughfare, preferring the comparatively quieter branch on the Vétheuil side of the islands.

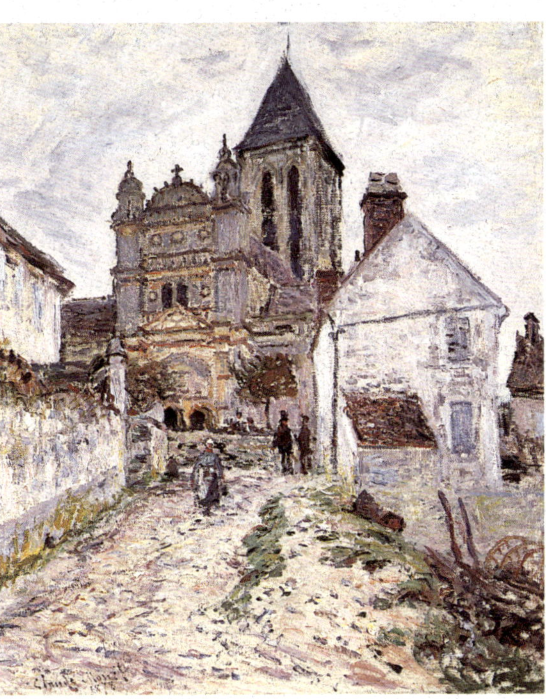

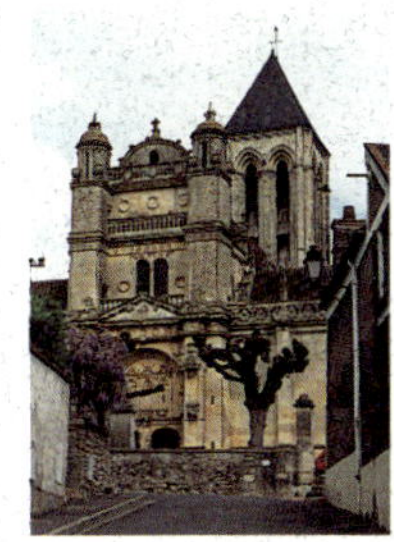

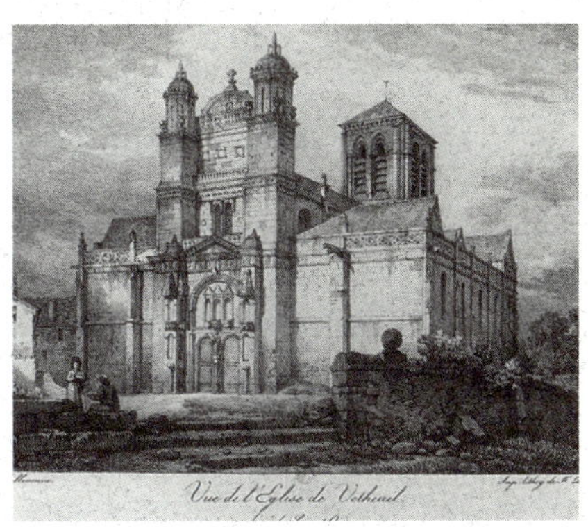

Fig. 3 (right)
Claude Monet
L'Eglise de Vétheuil
(The Church at Vétheuil)
1878
Oil on canvas
W. 474
National Gallery of Scotland

Fig. 4
(far right, above)
Church of Notre-Dame, Vétheuil
Photograph by the author

Fig. 5
(far right, below)
Louis Jules Frédéric Villeneuve
Vue de l'église de Vétheuil
(View of the Church of Vétheuil)
1819
Lithograph
Département des estampes et de la photographie, Bibliothèque nationale de France, Paris

Among Monet's earliest Vétheuil paintings is a pair of views of the town's chief object of historical and visual interest, the thirteenth-century church of Notre-Dame (W. 473-474; *L'Église de Vétheuil* is shown in fig. 3) which, like the town, has changed remarkably little since Monet lived there (fig. 4). The church had figured prominently in guidebooks and earlier writings about Vétheuil as the most prominent and ancient structure in the small town. It had also been featured in drawings and prints in the eighteenth and nineteenth centuries, including a lithograph by Louis Jules Frédéric Villeneuve (1796-1842) earlier in the century (fig. 5). The minutiae of the church's facade are carefully observed in Villeneuve's depiction; however, Monet concerns himself not with the details of the facade but rather with the massing of grays and blues as the church meets the steep recession of the street ascending to the tiny square in front of the church.

Monet had occasionally painted the same scene in pairs, dating back to early views of Honfleur and Paris from the 1860s, and this procedure was employed again in the paired views of the church.[9] As with the paired views of Paris dating from 1867, Monet was again exploring the possibilities of the same motif seen in vertical and horizontal formats. Although Monet had painted canvases of churches previously, from Barbizon images such as *La Chapelle de Notre-Dame de Grâce, Honfleur* (W. 35), which demonstrates his close kinship to Jongkind,[10] to the urban setting of the Parisian church of *St-Germain-l'Auxerrois* (W. 84), those churches had always appeared within the context of their surroundings, either rural or urban.[11] However, the two paintings of Notre-Dame are unlike any of his other views of churches until the 1890s. With their concentration on the facade, albeit at some distance, these early paintings of the church at Vétheuil clearly look forward to the Rouen Cathedral series executed in 1892-1893 (fig. 6). In the Rouen paintings, the facade of the cathedral fills the entire field and the distance between the motif and the viewer is collapsed. Monet's discrete Vétheuil pairing would be multiplied at Rouen into a vast ensemble of thirty canvases, each of which explores the atmospheric and coloristic nuances of that Gothic edifice, and which collectively created a truly symphonic response to the single motif, recording the most ephemeral modulations of color and shadow as light played across the facade.

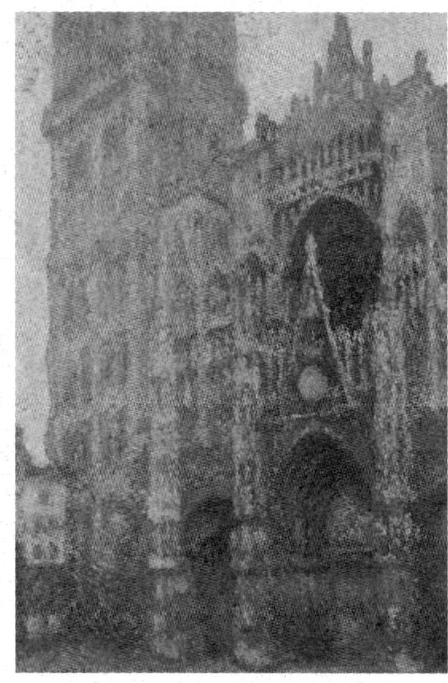

Fig. 6
Claude Monet
Portail de la cathédrale de Rouen, temps gris
(The Portal of the Rouen Cathedral, Gray Weather)
1894
Oil on canvas
W. 1345
Musée des Beaux-Arts, Rouen

Monet's continuing financial difficulties at Vétheuil resulted in a somewhat unorthodox living arrangement. Ernest Hoschedé, Monet's close friend and patron and an enthusiastic collector of Impressionist paintings, and his wife Alice merged households with Monet at Vétheuil, both families inhabiting the same house on the north end of town. The relationship between the families, particularly between Monet and Alice Hoschedé, became the subject of speculation and gossip, culminating in a mean-spirited attack in *Le Gaulois* in January 1880. Alice and Monet's wife Camille each gave birth to sons in late 1877 and early 1878 (with the suggestion by some that Monet was father to both children).[12] Camille became gravely ill, apparently during or just after the birth of Michel, her painful affliction initially diagnosed as an ulceration of the uterus. This malady, believed to be uterine cancer, proved a long and ultimately terminal illness, one that dominated the affairs of the Monet-Hoschedé household for the first year at Vétheuil.

During the spring and summer of 1879 Monet created a number of views of the orchards near his house, views of the town from the Lavacourt side of the river (pl. 9), and also two paintings which are reminiscent of his pastoral views from Argenteuil, *The Meadow* (W. 535, Dixon fig. 4) and *Poppy Field near Vétheuil* (W. 536, fig. 7). As Wildenstein observes, the cheerfulness of these two paintings belies the desperate sit-

Fig. 7
Claude Monet
Champ de coquelicots près de Vétheuil
(Poppy Field near Vétheuil)
Ca. 1880
Oil on canvas
W. 536
Foundation E.G. Bührle Collection, Zürich

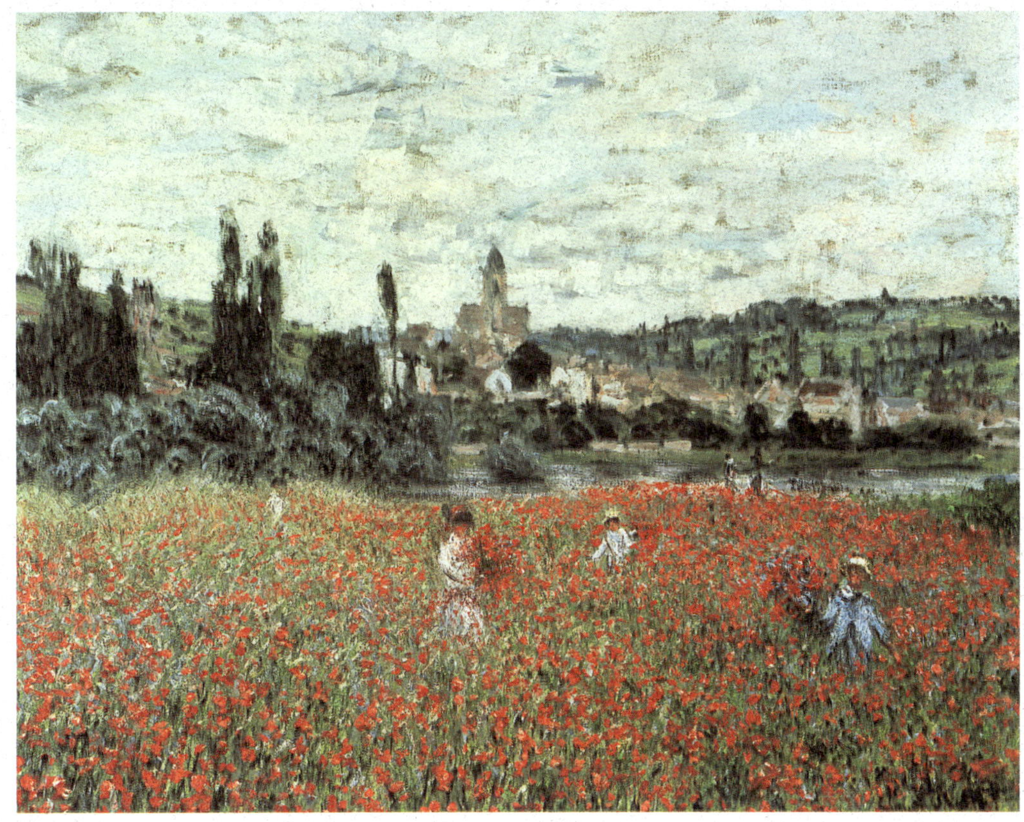

uation affecting the household.[13] The weather had been oppressive; Monet was unable to produce any work that satisfied him. Camille and baby Michel were both still quite ill, to the grave concern of everyone. Finances were at a critical juncture; Monet was so desperate for funds that in August he wrote in despair to his friend and patron Dr. Georges de Bellio, pleading that he go to Monet's studio in Paris and select some paintings to purchase.[14] Seen against this tortured backdrop, the two paintings of figures strolling through a meadow and gathering poppies on the islands in the river seem to be a denial of the artist's true situation.

However, a more personal drama may be present in the *Poppy Field near Vétheuil.* Camille's health by the spring was so poor that she could not leave the house; it may be presumed that the figures in this peaceful and idyllic painting are Alice and the combined Hoschedé and Monet children.[15] Since Alice may now have taken over Camille's role of model in this *plein-air* painting, it could signal the transfer of Monet's affections from his wife to Alice Hoschedé. There is no clear indication as to when Alice and Monet's feelings for one another moved beyond the platonic; however, it is possible to see the *Poppy Field near Vétheuil* as a reprise of Monet's famous painting of 1873 (fig. 8) showing Camille and Jean Monet in a field of poppies near Argenteuil. The earlier painting was produced in a time of greater prosperity and domestic felicity; this painting may well be an invocation of the "better days" that Monet alluded to in his letter to de Bellio; Monet had awaited in vain the return of those better days. Thus the *Poppy Field near Vétheuil* might have more to do with Monet's relationship with Camille than with Alice; perhaps it was Monet's farewell to Camille, substituting Alice in Camille's stead since Camille was no longer able to serve as a model. Alice would not be prominently featured again in Monet's work for a full year. Monet's most anguished and wrenching leave-taking, of course, was the deathbed portrait of Camille painted in early September of that year (pl. 10).

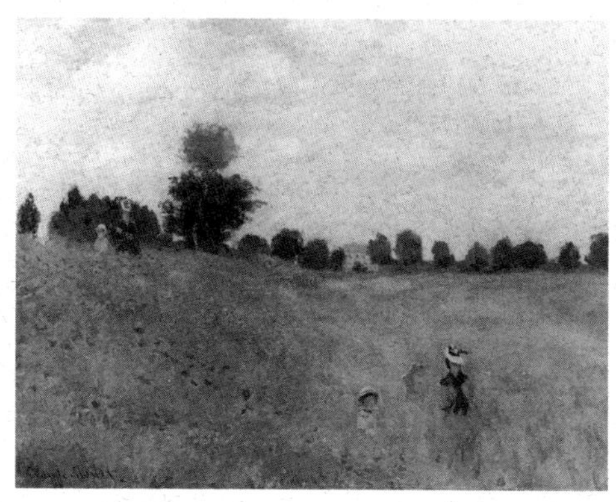

Fig. 8
Claude Monet
Les Coquelicots à Argenteuil
(Poppies at Argenteuil)
1873
Oil on canvas
W. 274
Musée d'Orsay, Paris

Monet has been described by critics in this century as an astute observer of natural phenomena—a viewpoint summed up in Cézanne's oft-quoted remark that Monet was "just an eye, but what an eye."[16] He has been considered an artist who observed and painted directly from nature. Scenes of modern life occupied him early in his career, and later he focused with greater concentration on the delicate transitions of light and color found in landscape. In his essay for the exhibition in June 1880 at the galleries of *La Vie Moderne*, Monet's good friend and critic Théodore Duret lauded just this aspect of *plein-air* directness in Monet's art. Citing the precedent of Corot and Courbet as artists who established the *plein-air* technique, Duret set up the tension between the fresh and spontaneous sketch executed on the spot and the final painting finished in the studio. He saw Monet as the artist whose paintings, begun and finished before the motif, eliminate the distance between sketch (*ébauche*) and tableau.[17]

It has been suggested that this image of Monet working his canvas to completion in the landscape was a myth that the artist carefully crafted over the years through interviews with the press, insisting that his paintings were not finished in the studio.[18] Even in his later years at Giverny, Monet perpetuated the belief that he was above all a *plein-air* painter; he was quoted by Lilla Cabot Perry as having said that he wished he had been born blind and given sight suddenly so that he could "see" without prior knowledge of his subject.[19] In fact, Monet did work up his paintings indoors, bringing the initial "impression" into greater finish and adjusting the chromatic and color balances within the work.[20] Although Monet did not have a formal studio at Vétheuil, there was the possibility of working in other rooms within the house, the attic and his own room.[21] It was during the years at Vétheuil that Monet's nascent serial technique was developed around the *Débâcle* paintings; sketches could be worked into more complete final form (e.g. W. 567, pl. 5, and W. 576, Dixon fig. 2), and variants could be developed from a painting executed on site. All of this fine-tuning in the studio would lead, in the fully developed series of the 1890s, to his method of ranging the related pictures around the room and adding the final touches to the ensemble.[22]

The traditional image of Monet as a superb observer of the natural world, a fantastic retinal organ that simply painted nature as it presented itself to him, does not hold up under closer examination.[23] Monet consciously selected portions of the landscape before him: in short, he edited his views of the site. Not only did he select the "view" from the sweep of the landscape before him, he also was selective as to what elements within the "view" were then included. Robert L. Herbert's recent examination of Monet's painting campaigns on the channel coast explores precisely this selectivity in Monet's paintings of Étretat, Pourville, and the other locales the painter visited along the coasts of Normandy and Brittany.[24] Monet had catered to the expectations of a leisure-based audience earlier, in his paintings of the 1860s and 1870s, beginning with *La Grenouillère* and including the regattas at Argenteuil.[25] This interest in fashionable recreation coincides with the depictions of these pastimes in the popular press. Yet

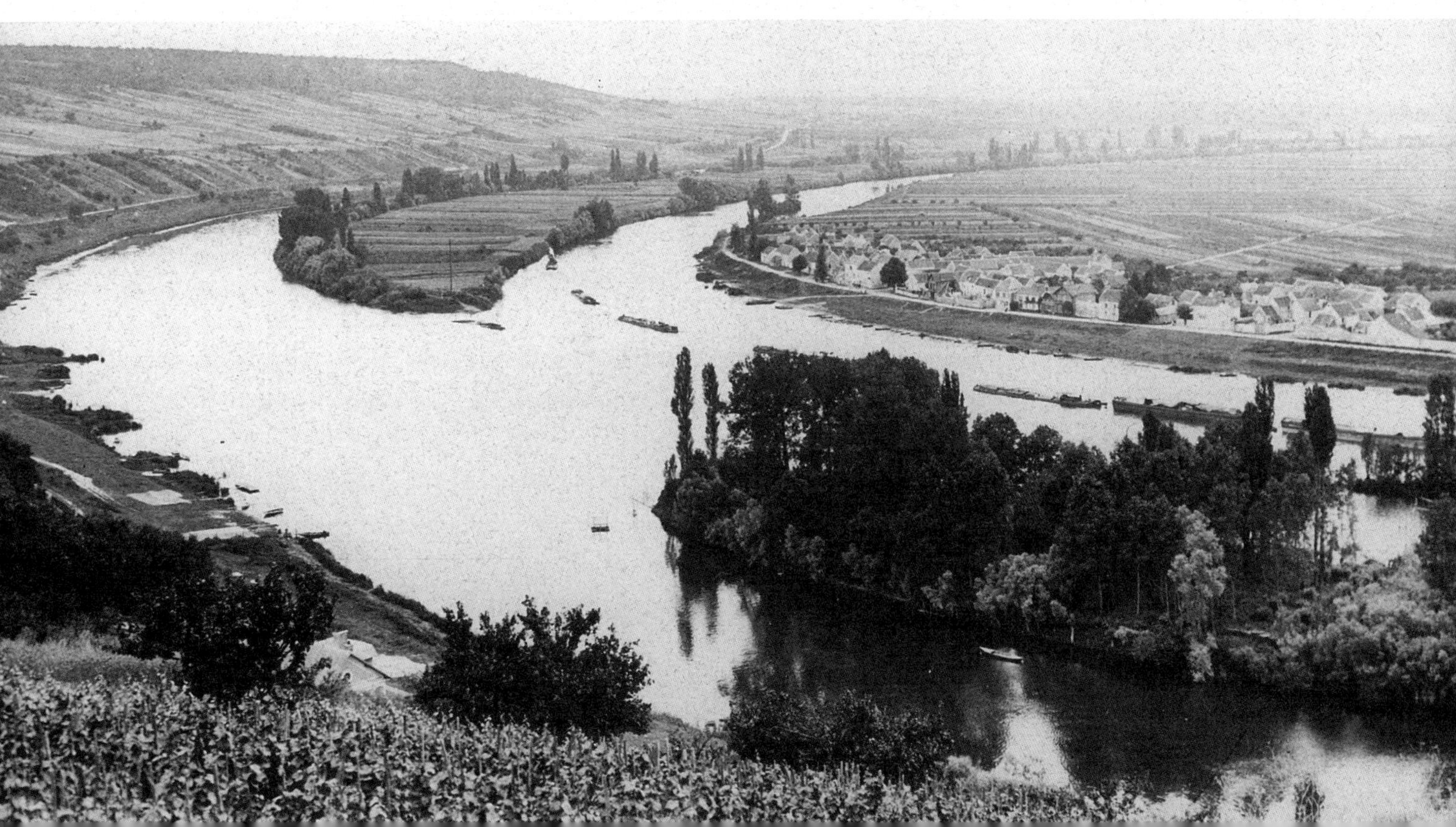

Fig. 9
Boucle de la Seine, Val d'Oise
(Bend of the Seine, Oise Valley [looking towards Lavacourt])
Ca. 1900
Roger-Viollet, Paris, cap. 17

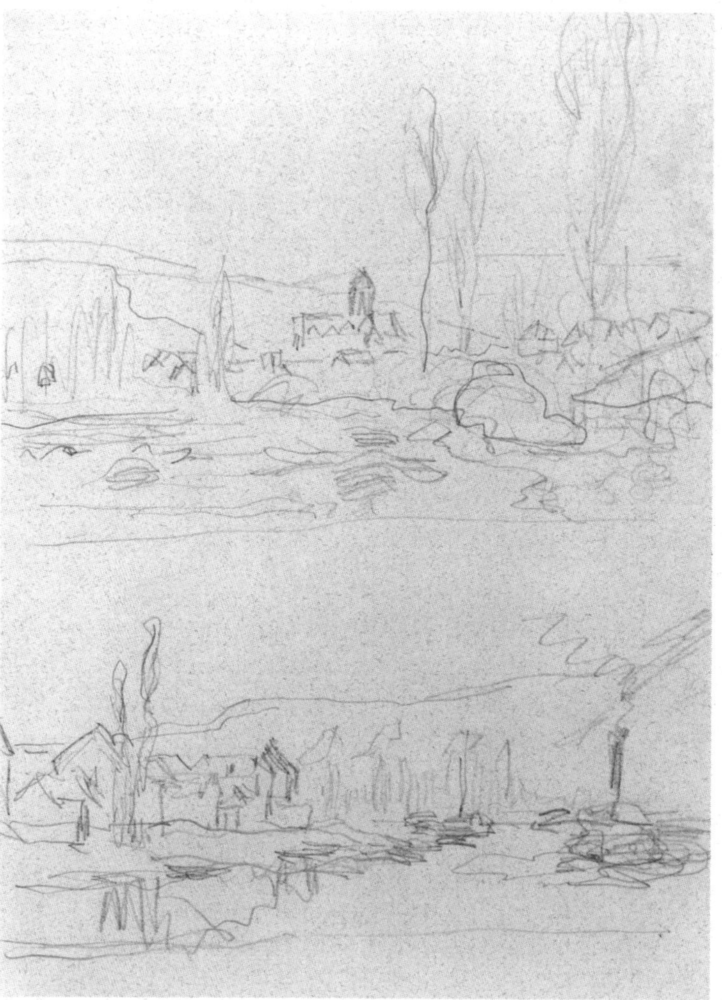

Fig. 10
Claude Monet
Deux esquisses: Vétheuil vue depuis l'île Saint-Martin. Remorqueurs devant Lavacourt (carnet de dessin, p. 35)
(Two Sketches: Vétheuil Seen from Île Saint Martin. Tugboats at Lavacourt [sketch book, p. 35])
Before 1886
Graphite
Musée Marmottan, Paris.

other factors shaped Monet's "view" as well. Knowing that Monet excluded some elements of his "view" in order to focus on others should permit another look at the subject matter of the Vétheuil paintings prior to the *Débâcles* of the winter of 1879-1880.

That Monet excluded certain obvious features of his environment becomes evident as the paintings are examined for alterations and omissions.[26] Some of the most startling exclusions include the very limited references to the presence of river traffic along the Seine, particularly barges and the tugs which directed boats along the river's shipping channels. Even though the Seine was one of the primary arteries for the transportation of goods through the western half of France, Monet's paintings of it, depicting both Lavacourt and Vétheuil, include very few canvases (e.g. W. 495, W. 501, and W. 517) in which there is any reference to this vital aspect of the river. Barge traffic on the Seine was an inescapable component of life along the river, as can be seen in a photograph of Lavacourt from the hills adjacent to Vétheuil (fig. 9). In this panorama a veritable train of barges moves through the primary channel on the Lavacourt side of the islands of Saint-Martin and Moisson. That Monet should so systematically exclude those ever-present emblems of contemporary commerce indicates that they were at odds with the images of Vétheuil and Lavacourt that he wished to present. It is clear that Monet was not totally oblivious of the day-to-day realities surrounding his new home, as can be seen from a drawing in the lower half of a page from Monet's *carnets* that depicts Lavacourt at the left and the smokestack of a tug silhouetted against the hills of Chantemesle to the right (fig. 10).

Barge traffic is not the only facet of river life that is edited out of these paintings. Monet excluded from his imagery all reference to the municipal passenger ferry that crossed between Vétheuil and Lavacourt.[27] As the conduit across the river in the absence of nearby bridges over the Seine, the ferry continued to be a focus in images of both towns, as can be seen in postcards dating from the turn of the century (figs. 11-13).

Why would Monet so drastically alter the presentation of these towns and their relationship to the Seine? What is lost in the elimination of the barges and ferry? What is gained in the portrayal of those river scenes without the commercial references? A major part of what is lost is the sense of these towns as vital participants in the life of contemporary France. Instead of bustling with economic concerns, they seem more rural than they in fact were; although the presence of man is implied in the views of Vétheuil and Lavacourt, figures rarely intrude in

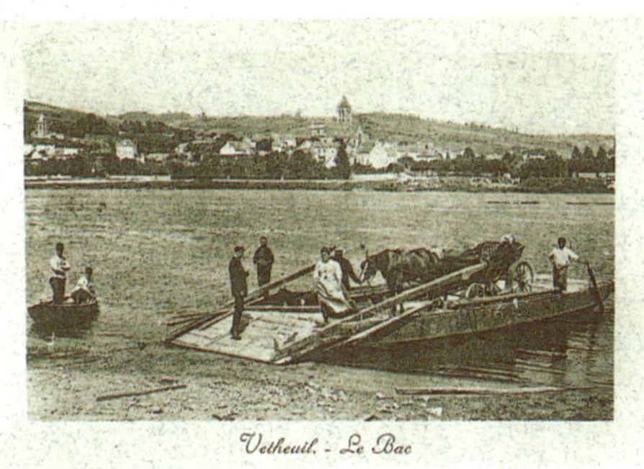

Fig. 11 (upper)
Vétheuil. Le Bac
(The Ferry at Vétheuil)
Postcard ca. 1900
Courtesy of the Archives of the Wildenstein Institute, Paris

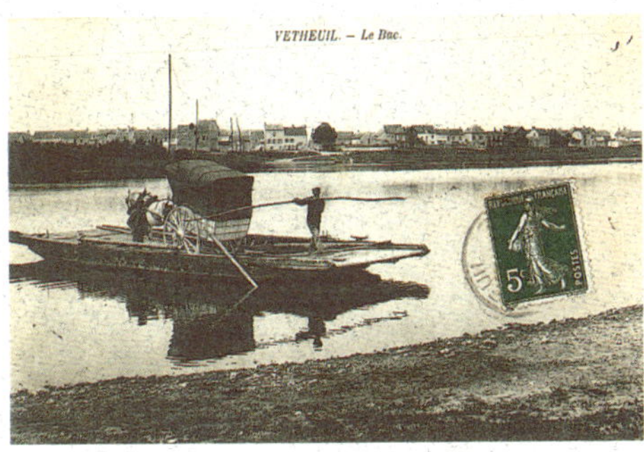

Fig. 12 (center)
Vétheuil—Le Bac
(The Ferry at Vétheuil)
Postcard ca. 1900
Courtesy of the Archives of the Wildenstein Institute, Paris

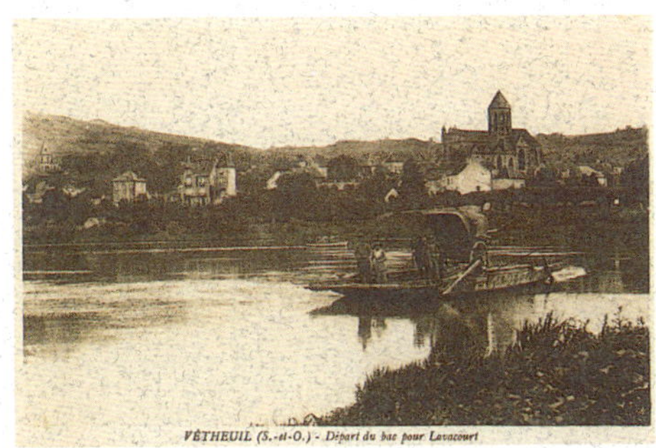

Fig. 13 (lower)
Départ du bac pour Lavacourt
(Departure of the Ferry to Lavacourt)
Postcard ca. 1900
Courtesy of the Archives of the Wildenstein Institute, Paris

the landscapes. This marks a distinct departure from the element of Monet's imagery that had been celebrated by Émile Zola, in his 1868 essay *Mon Salon*. Zola saluted Monet as a painter *par excellence* of modern life: he loves to paint the pastimes of men and women, their race courses, aristocratic promenades, women's umbrellas and gloves. In Monet's choice of landscape motifs he prefers an English park to a corner of the forest, and the artist cannot help but put the presence of man in the landscape.[28]

If the focus on contemporary French life has been deleted from these landscapes and riverscapes, what then did Monet choose to emphasize? One element that is retained is the fisherman's boat. Solitary in their pursuits, fishermen animate the stretches of water that occupy the foregrounds and middle grounds of the paintings of both towns. Did Monet in fact trade his earlier subject matter for subjects that revisited the paintings of the preceding generation? The paintings of Argenteuil, a recreation center so easily accessible to Parisians, might have had a ready-made clientele in Paris. The same may be true of the dramatic paintings of the Normandy coast, which was also a popular spot for vacationers. However, Monet portrayed Vétheuil and Lavacourt as agrarian hamlets removed from the *force majeur* of industrial society and modern life; there would not be an immediate audience for these paintings as souvenirs for Parisians back from holiday. The views of Vétheuil and Lavacourt, although so precisely observed as to time of day and weather, take on a timeless, elegiac aspect.

Claude Monet, in his representations of Lavacourt and Vétheuil, looked back to the roots of the Impressionist style; the quiet fishing hamlets which he recreated by excluding the modern and commercial traffic along the river evoke earlier Barbizon paintings by artists such as Rousseau and Charles Daubigny. Daubigny, who frequently painted the Seine between Paris and Rouen and even stayed at Vétheuil, owned a *botin*, a floating studio-boat, which allowed him to set his easel to capture any section of the river that caught his interest.[29] Following the older painter's example, Monet also had a studio-boat that allowed him to explore the riverbank. Initially having employed it at Argenteuil, Monet brought his studio-boat to Vétheuil and moored it at the bottom of his yard, which extended to the riverbank. These links to a Romantic past lead us into another component of Monet's painting, one which will dominate the *Débâcles* and continue to be vital to his paintings henceforth: the Romantic invocation of the sublime and terrible forces of nature.

THE WINTER OF 1879-1880 AND THE *DÉBÂCLES*

Bad weather intensified the gloom of the months following Camille's death in September of 1879. Unable to paint out-of-doors, Monet undertook a series of still lifes. Images of both dead game (pl. 12) and of fruit (pl. 11), known in French as *nature morte*, occupied Monet during the late fall, resulting in some of his most marketable paintings of the period. As winter approached the temperature plummeted in France and the rest of Europe. The weather became a regular news feature in the periodicals and newspapers of Paris. Once the Seine and other rivers in France froze over, the extreme weather conditions were exacerbated by a very brief thaw in late December, followed by a rapid and massive thaw on January 3, 1880. The snow run-off and the cascading ice that accumulated as the Seine's thick layer of ice broke apart resulted in massive devastation. Monet, invigorated by this once-in-a-lifetime surge of ice floes, created a memorable sequence of paintings to capture the river in its frozen immobility as well as its surging floods and blocks of ice. As observed above in connection with his use of prints showing fashionable recreation, Monet, like the other Impressionists, was quite familiar with the modes of representation in the popular press of the time.[30] Did Monet again capitalize on a popular and accessible means of documenting this exceptional winter, adapting the imagery in periodicals such as *La Nature* and *Le Monde*

Fig. 14
Meelon Tilly, after Férat
Aspect d'une rue le 14 Décembre
(View of a Street, December 14)
Wood engraving
La Nature, 1880, 1st semester, p. 57

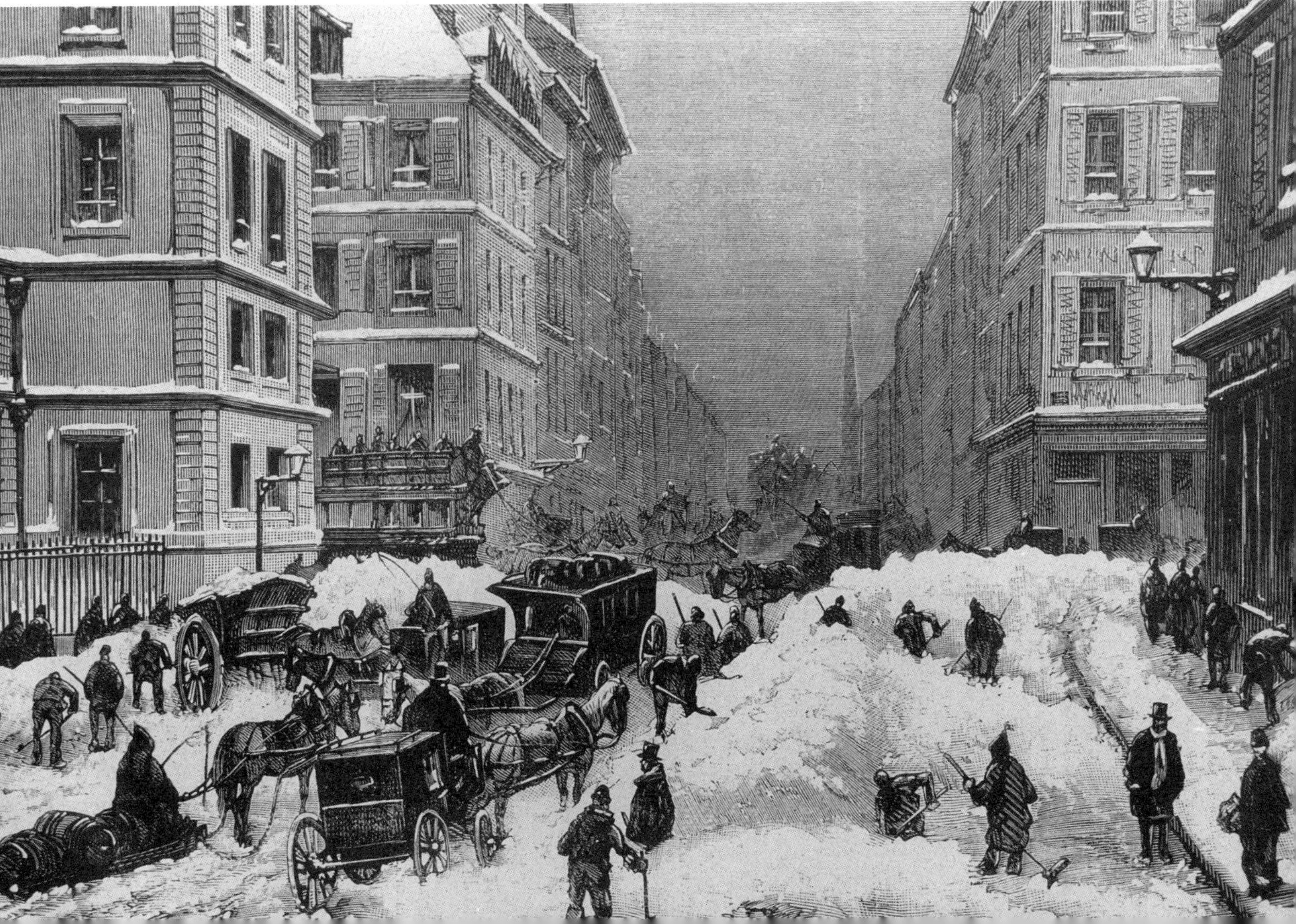

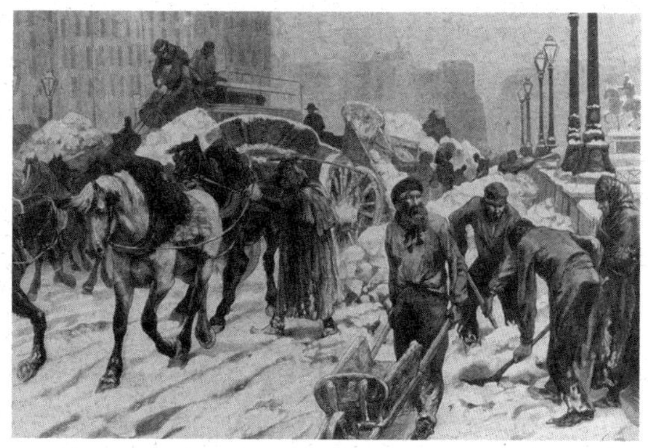

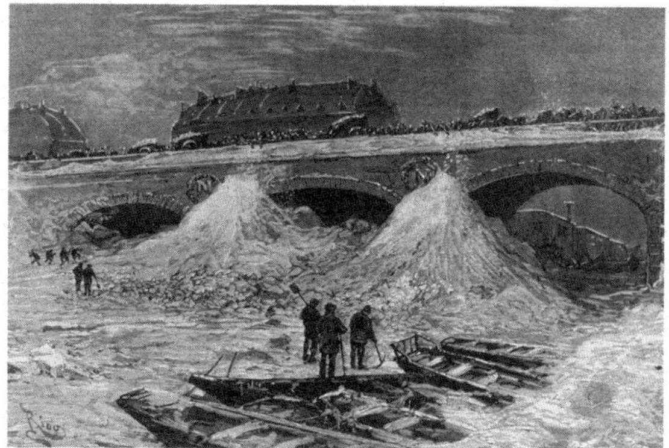

Fig. 15 (left)
Charles Baude, after Eugène Burnand
Le déchargement des tombereaux de neige dans la Seine—Vue prise sur le Pont-Neuf
(The Unloading of the Snow into the Seine—View from the Pont-Neuf)
Wood engraving
L'Illustration LXXIV, no. 1922 (December 27, 1879), p. 404

Fig. 16 (right)
Riou, after L. Dumont
L'hiver à Paris.—L'amoncellement des neiges sur la Seine au Pont Saint-Michel
(Winter in Paris—The Accumulation of Snow on the Seine near the Pont Saint-Michel)
Wood engraving
L'Illustration LXXIV, no. 1922 (December 27, 1879), p. 408

illustré, or did he in fact create a completely different response in his images of the upheaval of great masses of ice in the Seine? An examination of how the severe cold weather and subsequent breakup of the ice choking the Seine were portrayed in the Paris press will allow an assessment of Monet's achievement.

The winter of 1879-1880 was one of the coldest and most severe that had been recorded in the nineteenth century; it was compared with the privations experienced during the winters of 1870-1871 and particularly 1830-1831, when the Seine had similarly frozen.[31] The autumn weather that had forced Monet to work indoors became worse throughout November; in mid-November the temperature fell below freezing and remained there with almost no relief until the warming trend in early January that resulted in the inundation of ice and water that overran the banks of the Seine. The bitterest cold of the winter was experienced during the first fifteen days of December, with temperatures reaching minus 25.6 degrees C. on December 10.[32] The snow began in earnest November 29 and continued off and on all through December; the accumulated snow was so deep that it brought transportation around the city and across the country almost to a halt as roads were rendered impassable and trains were unable to transport goods into Paris (see fig. 14).[33] Fuel and food supplies began to run short. The river began to form a skin of ice on December 6 and within a few days had reached a thickness of ten to twelve centimeters, eventually reaching a thickness in some places of forty or fifty centimeters, thick enough to "support veritable mountains of snow and ice."[34] The snow removal required the mobilization of thousands of workers who brought immense cartloads of snow from around the city in order to dispose of them from the bridges and quays on top of the already frozen river (figs. 15 and 16). The snow piled up in such mounds around the bridges that someone took advantage of the hillocks of ice and snow to decorate the Pont-Royal with graffiti in places other-

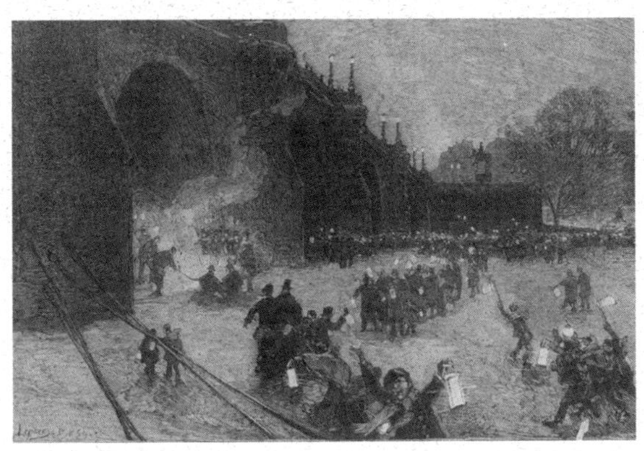

Fig. 17 (above)
Auguste Lepère
Paris sous la neige.—Le Réveillon sur la glace au Pont-Neuf
(Paris under the Snow.—Christmas Revelers on the Ice near the Pont-Neuf)
Wood engraving
Le Monde illustré XLVI, no. 1188 (January 3, 1880), p. 4

Fig. 18 (below)
Gaston Vuillier
Au bord de la Seine—Buvette groënlandaise
(On the Bank of the Seine—Greenland Drinking Room)
Wood engraving
Le Monde illustré XXIII, no. 1187 (December 27, 1879), p. 408

wise inaccessible.[35] The December 13 edition of *Le Figaro* told of health concerns raised by the refuse buried in the snow.[36]

In the face of mounting concerns, Parisians' response to the worsening conditions in the city, and journalists' manner of reporting the protracted cold and snow, took several different directions. First, there was the delight and fascination at the exceptional conditions in the city; skaters were to be found on the lake in the Bois de Boulogne and in other public gardens, and on the Seine, taking their chances and risking falling through in thin spots. *La Nature* reported that on Christmas Day there were thousands of people seen crossing the ice on the Seine until the police intervened (fig. 17).[37] Reports on the conditions in Paris included observations of the novelty and beauty of the city's trees covered in the frost of mid-December.[38] Certainly one of the most inventive uses for the vast amounts of snow was the "igloo" constructed by an enterprising Parisian near the Hôtel-de-Ville known as the Greenland drinking room—"la buvette groënlandaise"[39] (fig. 18).

In contrast to these light-hearted, even frivolous, responses to the cold weather, the majority of the commentaries in the press regarding the severe winter dealt with hardships, damage, and loss to property, and apprehensions about the inevitable flood that would occur once the snow and ice melted. *Le Figaro* noted that "It is always towards the Seine that the public turns its thoughts."[40] A certain siege mentality settled in; fears were expressed about possible famine and outbreaks of disease. The government took steps to minimize the anticipated effects of the thaw, including dynamiting the ice near the Pont des Invalides, under reconstruction at the time. Predictions of the thaw began in late December, although it was not until the night of January 2 that the temperatures began to rise and the *dégel*, or rapid thaw, set in motion a series of events that demonstrated just how destructive the powers of nature could be. These reports culminated in the detailed descriptions and wood engravings of the *débâcle* that began in Paris on January 3.

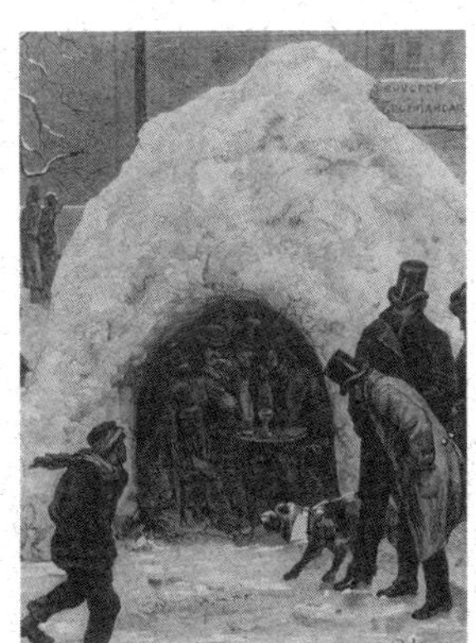

The days leading up to the thaw were filled with suspense and a feeling of impending doom. *Le Figaro* published a series of articles detailing the ravages of previous *débâcles*, voicing concern about the rising temperatures, and fretting over the weakened state of the Pont des Invalides.[41] In an effort to protect the Pont des Invalides and the temporary wooden footbridge constructed while the bridge was undergoing restoration, the authorities tried dynamiting the ice between the Pont de la Concorde and the Pont de Solférino in late December, drawing large crowds along the embankments to watch as the charges were set off to dislodge the ice (fig. 19). The *passerelle*, or footbridge, had developed a crack in mid-December and the amount of ice piling up on the piers of both it and the bridge were of great concern to authorities. These efforts to dislodge the ice with dynamite were not enough to save either structure once the waters rose.

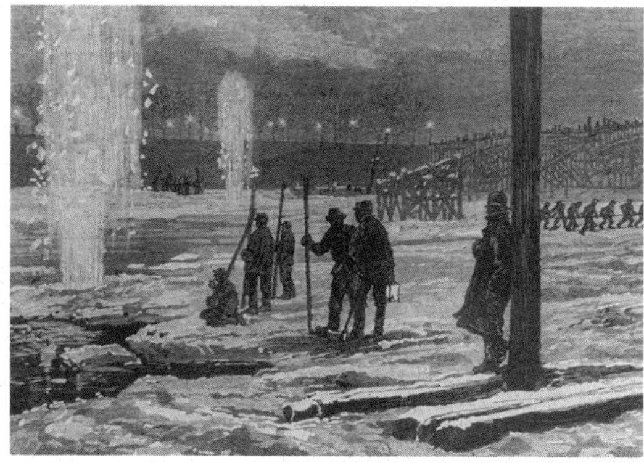

Fig. 19
W. Toller, after Kauffmann
Paris sous la neige.—Rupture de la glace au moyen de la dynamite au pont des Invalides
(Paris under the Snow.—Dynamiting the Ice near the Pont des Invalides)
Wood engraving
Le Monde illustré XLVI, no. 1188 (January 3, 1880), p. 4

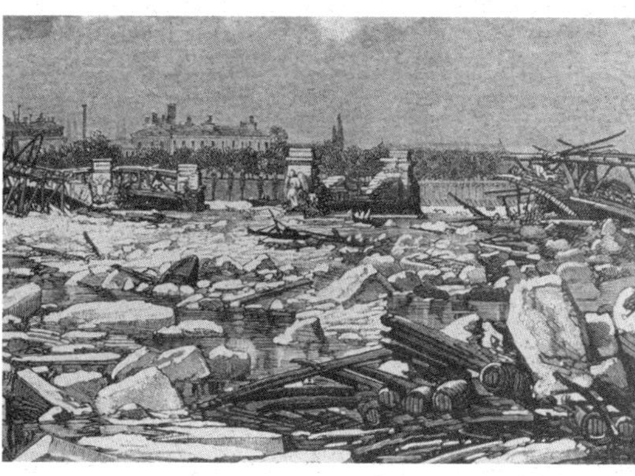

Fig. 20
Meelon Tilly, after Tisser
La débâcle de la Seine. Aspect du pont des Invalides écroulé le 3 janvier 1880
(The Breakup of the Ice on the Seine. The Pont des Invalides Collapsed, January 3, 1880)
Wood engraving
La Nature, no. 347 (January 24, 1880), p. 116

The breakup of the ice in the Seine at Paris, when it came, was spectacular. The thaw began on January 2, but reached its peak the morning of January 3. Gaston Tissandier, writing in *La Nature*, described the unfolding events. At 7 p.m. on the night of January 2 the central portion of the *passerelle* had been demolished, and throughout the night the destruction continued so that by morning little trace of the *passerelle* remained. At 10 a.m. the next morning the ice began to break apart, piling up against any obstacle in its path. Along the piers of Paris's bridges the ice accumulated with thunderous blows. Crowds thronged the quays and watched the destruction while the water rose one and a half meters between 10 a.m. and 1 p.m., and continued rising. The shocks and blows of the ice and debris against the piers of the Invalides proved too much; by 1:50 p.m. the two central arches of the bridge had been washed away (fig. 20).[42]

Over the next several days *Le Figaro* and other periodicals devoted a number of articles to the *débâcle* in Paris, detailing the damage to bridges across the city with illustrations such as those shown in fig. 21. The bridges were not the only elements of life along the river to suffer. As the water and ice surged downstream through Paris they carried away boats, barges, and other debris, breaking them apart and battering them against the piers of bridges downstream (figs. 22 and 23). One barge filled with timber

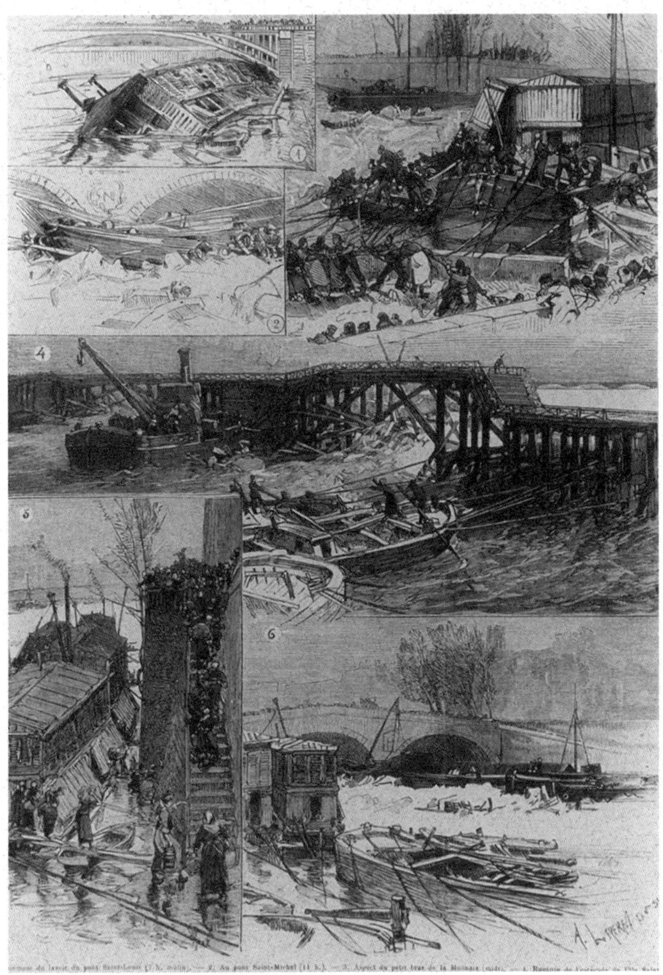

Fig. 21
Auguste Lepère
Paris.—La grande Débâcle de la Seine du 3 janvier.—Du pont d'Austerlitz au Pont-Neuf
(Paris.—The Big Breakup of the Ice on the Seine, January 3.—From the Pont d'Austerlitz to the Pont-Neuf)
Wood engraving
Le Monde illustré XLVI, no. 1189 (January 10, 1880), p. 29

broke apart, sending enormous quantities of lumber cascading down the Seine along with the ice.[43]

The surge of ice and high water moved downstream to the suburbs and countryside. Many of the articles that summarized the *débâcle* in Paris also described the damage to towns along the Seine outside Paris and along other rivers in the country, including the Marne and Loire rivers. Throughout the country, severe flooding was observed, including extensive damage to the poplars that stood along the banks of the Marne, snapping trees that measured forty centimeters in circumference. A boatbuilder had fallen into the Marne at the height of the *débâcle* and miraculously survived being crushed by the ice.[44] The ravaged countryside was captured in the periodicals (fig. 24) for Parisian readers.

Thus the city was described both in terms of the unique appearance of the frozen Seine, and also in terms of the hardships and shortages due to the severity of the temperatures and amount of snow accumulation. Paris was compared to St. Petersburg, and the Seine to the Neva,[45] and the descriptions often characterized the winter and, in particular, the thaw of January 3, with words such as "horror," "grandiose and terrifying," and referred to the "wrath of the elements."[46]

What transpired in Vétheuil as the surge of water and ice arrived in early January? How were Monet's immediate surroundings affected, and in what manner did Monet chose to depict the frozen Seine and the *débâcle*? In what ways do his paintings convey an experience of the winter different from that portrayed in the Paris press?

Vétheuil, like Paris, became snowbound in early December, and people could walk across the river between Vétheuil and Lavacourt. Monet, Alice, and the children spent a cold and bleak Christmas, apparently without Ernest Hoschedé's presence.

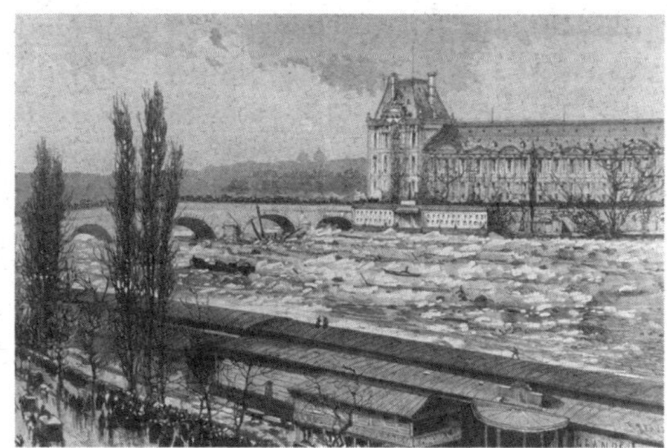

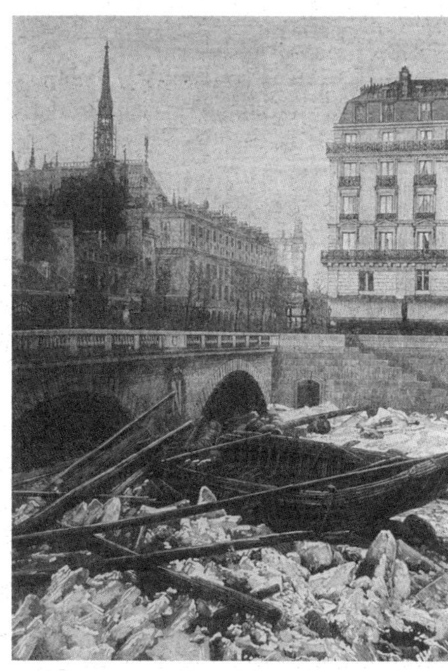

Fig. 22 (left)
E. Meaulle, after H. Scott
Paris.—La grande Débâcle du 3 janvier.—Aspect de la Seine, en amont du Pont-Royal, à 11 heures du matin
(Paris.—The Big Breakup of the Ice on the Seine, January 3.—The Seine, Upstream of the Pont-Royal at Eleven O'clock in the Morning)
Wood engraving
Le Monde illustré XLVI, no. 1189 (January 10, 1880), p. 28

Fig. 23 (right)
Godefroy
Une photographie de la débâcle, prise le 3 janvier, par M. Godefroy, en face du pont Saint-Michel
(Photograph of the Breakup of the Ice, January 3, Taken by M. Godefroy, Opposite the Pont Saint-Michel)
Wood engraving
Le Monde illustré XLVI, no. 1190 (January 17, 1880), p. 48

Whether his absence was due to tensions within the household or to his inability to get to Vétheuil is not clear.[47] Monet made a trip to Paris on December 28, having borrowed fifty francs from the postmistress of Vétheuil, in an attempt to sell some of his "Winter Effects."[48] That he would attempt this trip to the city in such cold and snow is a testament to his desperate financial situation. The trip had some measure of success, as Petit and Duret each bought a painting for a combined 450 francs. The brief thaw of late December was described by Alice the next day as "a terrifying thaw." "The whole mass of snow," she wrote, "is falling on us from the tops of the hills, the courtyard is flooded, the water will be inside the house if things continue, it's raining buckets."[49]

In the evening of January 4, with Ernest away in Paris, Monet, Alice, and the children retired for the night. At 9 p.m. the breakup reached the town of Mantes-la-Jolie and continued downstream to reach Vétheuil and Lavacourt before dawn on January 5. Immense amounts of ice were piling up in their area with the same tremendous effect as in Paris. As Alice described, "On Monday, at five in the morning, I was woken by a terrifying noise, like thunder; a few minutes later I heard Madeleine [the cook] knocking on M. Monet's window, telling him to get up. I immediately did the same, while the booming sound was mixed with cries coming from Lavacourt. I quickly ran to the window, and, dark as it was, I could see blocks of white falling; this time it was the real breakup of the ice floes."[50] After two hours the rush of ice began to subside. The devastation on the Vétheuil side was quite pronounced; trees were broken, and gardens along the river, including Monet's, were badly damaged. Later in the day the family rented a carriage to inspect the damage in the area; Wildenstein quotes a letter from Alice to Ernest, in which she describes the devastation as "heart-rending."[51] The debris left behind was significant; inhabitants of Lavacourt scavenged firewood from the flotsam left in nearby fields by the ice and waters, and there were reports of corpses floating on the river.

By January 8 Monet wrote to de Bellio that, "Here we have had a terrible *débâcle* and of course I tried to make something of it."[52] The paintings that Monet produced during this winter have a haunting, lonely quality that has sometimes been interpreted as continuing sorrow following the death of Camille earlier in the fall.[53] The paintings of the frozen river and *débâcle*, however, may not have indicated a mournful withdrawal. Monet may in fact simply have been responding to the extreme weather conditions. The last time that the Seine had frozen, in 1870-1871, had been during the Franco-Prussian War. Monet produced no similar paintings of the Seine dating from that winter, for he and Pissarro had spent it together in London, away from the war. But Monet had painted numerous winter scenes in other years prior to this record cold and snow.

Fig. 24

H. Scott, after Peaulot, Dick, and Materre

La Débâcle de la Seine et la Marne, en amont de Paris

(The Breakup of the Ice on the Seine and the Marne, Upstream of Paris)

Wood engraving

Le Monde illustré XLVI no. 1190 (January 17, 1880), p. 45

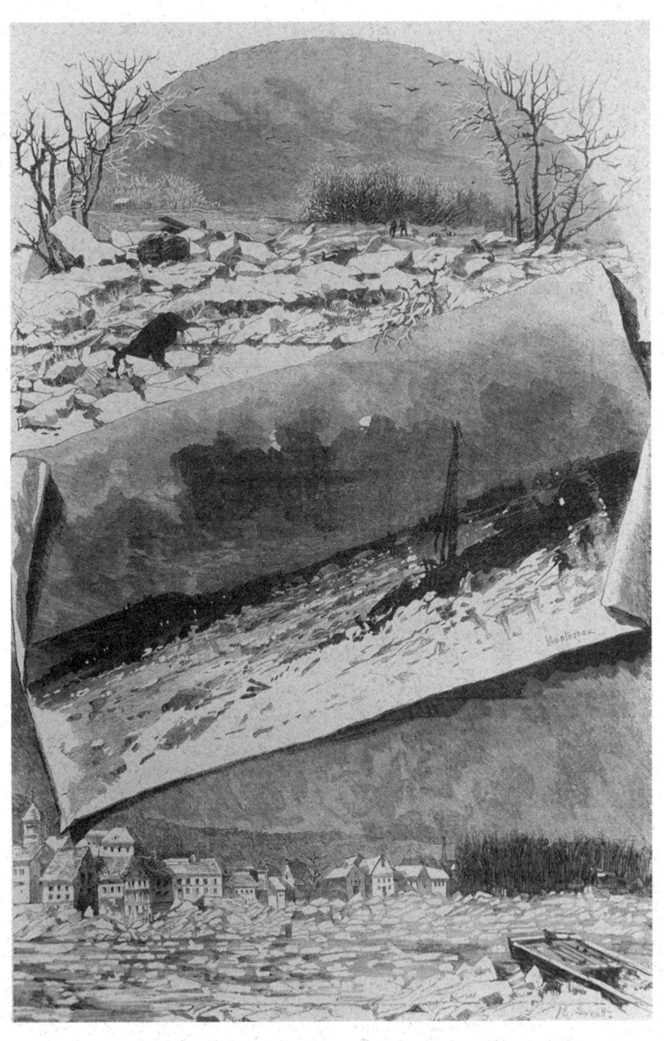

The paintings of the harsh winter at Vétheuil took the artist's winter landscapes in a new direction. Of the twenty-five works (W. 552-576) that comprise the winter paintings, very few of them include reference to human presence.[54] These paintings can be divided into two basic types: views of the frozen landscape painted in December prior to the thaw in early January, and those paintings, known as *Glaçons*, that depict the ice floes and their reflections after the thaw had broken up the ice on the Seine. In the backgrounds of the first paintings of the frozen river that winter, Vétheuil and Lavacourt can be seen silhouetted across the ice of the river. There are a few that include boats in the foreground (W. 553-556), begun most likely during the month of December, and one that has a standing or kneeling man maneuvering his boat between the ice floes (W. 573), which probably dates from sometime in late January or February.

The rest of the *glaçons* paintings concentrate on the interplay of light—often at sunset—on objects and their reflections on the water. These paintings have both a delicate nuance of atmosphere and a bold handling of color and paint.

These largely unpeopled paintings of the ice-filled Seine contrasted sharply with the depictions of the river in the Paris media, beginning with the onset of the cold in November through the breakup of the ice in early January. As we have seen, the portrayals of the Seine in Paris during the cold winter had been captured in wood engravings that showed the effect of the weather on the populace. These images were filled with people: crowds walking on the ice, shoveling the snow, watching as the torrents of water and ice battered the city's bridges. Readily accessible through the printed medium, they were filled with the salient details of the severe weather and its effect on the lives of the inhabitants of Paris. Like the articles in the publications which they accompanied, the prints essentially told a story. It is precisely this quality of implied narrative that is absent from Monet's paintings of the *glaçons*. Not unlike the painter's summer river views that lent his new home a more rural aspect that it actually had, these ice paintings also minimized the presence of people and eliminated the quality of storytelling that made the wood engravings, full of vivid detail, so descriptive.

Were there no images in the periodicals upon which Monet could draw for inspiration as he had in his use of fashion prints a decade before? It is possible that popular imagery could have again provided him with some general direction. The aforementioned painting of a man in a skiff or open boat navigating between the ice floes (W. 573, private collection, Netherlands) shows a figure using a pole to push the ice floes away from his boat. The canvas bears a striking resemblance to a wood engraving from *L'Illustration* depicting a group of men engaged in a similar activity, in particular the man to the left in the print (fig. 25). Both show the figure of a boatman

Fig. 25 (left)
Riou, after L. Dumont
La Débâcle de la Seine à Asnieres.–Vue prise de l'Île de la Grande-Jatte
(The Breakup of the Ice on the Seine.–View from the Island of the Grand-Jatte)
Wood engraving
L'Illustration LXXV, no. 1924 (January 10, 1880), p. 36

Fig. 26 (right)
Unknown artist
La débâcle de la Seine. Les derniers glaçons aux environs de Paris le 5 janvier 1880
(The Breakup of the Ice on the Seine. The Last Floes near Paris, January 5, 1880)
Wood engraving
La Nature, no. 347 (January 24, 1880), p. 117

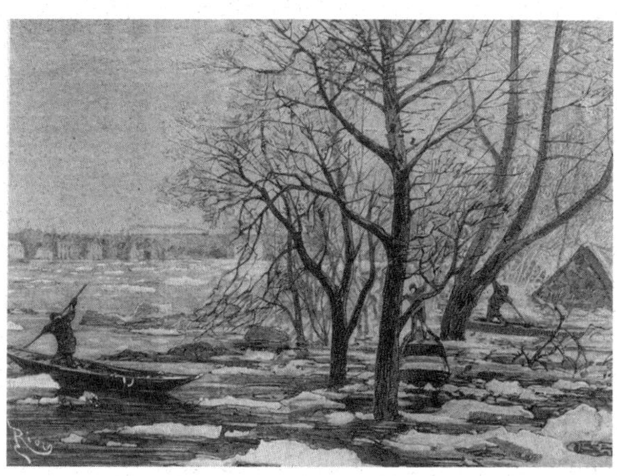

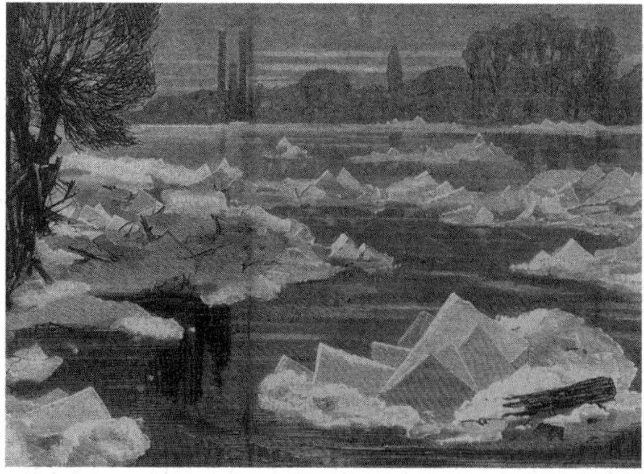

silhouetted against the background; the position of the man with his pole, and both the shape of the boat and its diagonal placement within the image, suggest a possible connection between the two.

Another compelling example, perhaps, is an illustration from *La Nature* in the wake of the breakup of the ice (fig. 26). Devoid of human presence except for the factory chimneys silhouetted against the sky, this remote and unpopulated view of the river is as stark as Monet's paintings of the same post-*débâcle* river, such as the paintings from Lisbon, Lille, and Dunedin (W. 560-562; the Dunedin painting is shown in pl. 2). Both the print from *La Nature* and Monet's paintings depict the same somber aspect of the river inundating the landscape, including the ice floes animating the surface of the water and the wreckage of trees framing the river under leaden, overcast skies.[55] It may be possible that Monet, so desperate for funds at the end of the year that he needed to borrow money to get to Paris to sell his paintings, could have believed that an audience in Paris might be receptive to a more poetic response to the *débâcle*. Consequently, he may have employed an image already familiar to readers of the periodicals in his own portrayal of the catastrophic thaw.

As has been frequently observed, Monet's *Débâcle* and *Glaçons* paintings do not form a cohesive series in the manner of the paintings of Rouen Cathedral or the poplars on the Epte river. They do form groupings that are clearly serial, however, and this method of working was becoming well-rooted in the paintings of Vétheuil.[56] If Monet was to capture the continually changing, never-to-be-repeated aspects of the river as the frozen Seine became a moving mountain of ice, he may have been forced to begin a number of studies in the cold and snow which he could expand upon later in the house or at his studio space on the rue Vintimille in Paris. Those paintings, initially begun outdoors, could then be reworked and completed away from the motif; variants could be made, or could be expanded to a larger scale, as with the Orsay *Glaçons* painting (pl. 5) and the larger Salon submission now at the Shelburne Museum (Dixon fig. 1).

Monet's paintings of the winter of 1879-1880 can be seen as an extension of the direction his painting had taken since his establishment at Vétheuil. His abandonment of the contemporary urban setting in favor of more rural, less suburban motifs can be seen again in the paintings of the frozen Seine. He provides no anecdotal portrayals of figures interacting with the elements; he depicts simply those elements themselves—water, ice, sky, hills—without the reference to their impact on mankind. The haunting quality of many of these paintings of the winter, from the more freely handled smaller paintings and the Petit Palais *Coucher de soleil* (Dixon fig. 2), to the more highly finished versions such as the Michigan and Shelburne paintings (pl. 3, Dixon fig. 1), seems to evoke associations with the Romantic sublime. Throughout his career, Monet always enjoyed the challenges involved with capturing severe weather and extraordinary effects of nature. He had painted winter scenes previously, as well as rough seas along the Normandy coast. In fact, the most important painting excursion Monet undertook from Vétheuil was to the Normandy coast in 1881, where he risked life and limb in rising tides to capture certain views of the sea. It would be landscape that remained his constant subject matter henceforth.

The three years that Monet spent in Vétheuil proved to be a critical juncture for him, personally and professionally. His family, now combined with that of Alice Hoschedé and her children—although not without complications in the intermittent presence and communications of Ernest—had become a permanent arrangement by the time they moved from Vétheuil to Poissy in the fall of 1881. The financial difficulties endured in the first years at Vétheuil finally eased after the success of the exhibition at *La Vie Moderne*. Monet's serial method of working would in the future dovetail beautifully with the one-man exhibitions, culminating over the next fifteen years in the critical successes of the established series paintings. The acknowledged painter of contemporary life who settled in Vétheuil in 1878 departed from that town in 1881, as from a chrysalis, renewed and redirected. He was no longer the painter of modernity who "preferred an English garden to a corner of the forest," as Zola had described him. Monet settled farther downriver at Giverny and, through his series paintings, created a whole new understanding of landscape painting. Many of those later innovations derived their impetus from the paintings executed of the ice-filled Seine.

Notes

I would like to give special thanks to my parents, whose visits to the Art Institute of Chicago imbued all their children with a love of art, and above all to my husband, Dennis, who was my most exacting and generous critic, and to my sons, Andrew and David, who, with patience and understanding, gave up our irreplaceable time together so that I could bring the project to completion.

1 Blanche Hoschedé recorded her recollections of Monet decades after his death. See Jean-Pierre Hoschedé, *Claude Monet, ce mal connu* (Geneva, 1960), 1:159.

2 See Paul Hayes Tucker. *Monet at Argenteuil*, (New Haven and London, 1982). This study of Monet's years at Argenteuil explores the artist's positioning as a painter of *la vie moderne* in his depictions of this popular weekend leisure town downriver from Paris.

3 Daniel Wildenstein, *Catalogue raisonné, Werkverzeichnis*, trans. Chris Miller, Peter Snowdon, and Josephine Bacon, 4 vols. (Cologne, 1996), 1:130-132.

4 Tucker 1982, 185.

5 Wildenstein 1996, 1:137. Unlike Argenteuil, which had a train station right at the town, it required greater effort to get to Vétheuil. After disembarking from the train at Mantes, travelers were then obliged to take M. Papavoine's "conveyance" the remaining 10-12 kilometers to Vétheuil.

6 There was an informal ferry service between Lavacourt and Vétheuil prior to 1870, when the municipality of Vétheuil organized a passenger ferry between the two towns. In 1884 the town upgraded the conveyance into a ferry that could transport carts as well as passengers. The new ferry began service in 1887; it is this latter service that was depicted in postcards from the turn of the century (figs. 11-13). My thanks to M. Claude A. Bonvalot, *Maire* of Moisson, and MM. Arnaud Ramière de Fortanier and Olivier Mijoint from the Archives Départementales des Yvelines, who provided much useful information about the Seine during Monet's years at this site.

7 Monet did occasionally return to vacation destinations or to other popular sites. This would imply a continuing interest in depicting resorts and leisure pursuits. For a discussion of aspects of tourism in Monet's paintings see Robert L. Herbert, *Monet and the Normandy Coast : Tourism and Painting, 1867-1886* (New Haven and London, 1994). For a discussion of the continuing Romantic vein in Monet's work and related issues of gender, see Norma Broude, *Impressionism: A Feminist Reading: the Gendering of Art, Science and Nature in the Nineteenth Century* (New York, 1991).

8 For a recent discussion of the role that the Seine played as a main artery for commercial traffic, as well as its role in the work of the Impressionists, see Richard Brettell, "The River Seine: Subject and Symbol in Nineteenth-Century French Art and Literature," in *Impressionists on the Seine*, exh. cat. Washington, The Phillips Collection, 1996 (Washington, 1996).

9 Monet's paintings of pairs harken back to the advice of his Barbizon predecessors, such as his teacher Johann Barthold Jongkind and Théodore Rousseau, who recommended to his students that they always take two canvases with them to record the same motif under different light conditions, one for morning and the other for evening. This working procedure could be further subdivided into as many canvases as needed to record ever smaller fleeting changes in the effects of light. Thus the serial paintings, which would become the hallmark of Monet's style beginning in the 1880s, are firmly grounded in the methods of the preceding generation of Barbizon painters. For discussion of Monet's paired paintings see Joel Isaacson, "Monet's Views of Paris," *Allen Memorial Art Museum Bulletin*, (Oberlin), 24, no. I, (Fall, 1966): 5-22, and Steven Levine, "Monet's Pairs," *Arts Magazine* 49, no. 10, (June 1975): 72-75. One early example is the pair of canvases depicting the rue de La Bavolle at Honfleur (W. 33-34) in which the scene is captured under the same lighting conditions, but with a different grouping of figures on the street. The views taken from the second-floor colonnade of the Louvre (W. 83, W. 85) depict Paris with the dome of the Pantheon dominating the horizon line; one canvas is vertically oriented, the other horizontally.

Charles Stuckey also sees the early pair of paintings of the church of Notre-Dame as a precedent for the series of Rouen Cathedral; see Chicago, The Art Institute of Chicago, *Claude Monet, 1840-1926*, exh. cat., Charles Stuckey (Chicago, 1995), 203.

10 See Broude 1991, 42-43.

11 Other churches figure in his views of towns, for instance at Sainte-Adresse (W. 98); most of his views of Vétheuil include Notre-Dame; and later at Varengeville (W. 725-728), and Vernon (W. 1386-1391), also at San Giorgio Maggiore and Santa Maria della Salute in Venice, he turned again to churches.

12 Stuckey, 201-202. Alice Hoschedé gave birth to Jean-Pierre in August of 1877; Camille Monet gave birth to Michel the following March. Monet had been invited to paint at the Hoschedés' estate at Rottenbourg the previous year. With Ernest away on business, it is possible that Alice and Monet might have had an affair during that visit.

13 See Wildenstein 1996, 1: 141-142, 145; see also letters, Daniel Wildenstein, *Claude Monet: Biographie et catalogue raisonné*, 5 vols. (Lausanne, 1974-1991), 1: 437, L. 158-160, dating from May 14 and May 28, 1879.

14 Letter to de Bellio, dated August 17, Wildenstein 1974, 1: 437, L. 161. The poignancy of Monet's situation is conveyed in the opening lines, "For a long time I have hoped for better days, alas, but today I must, I believe, give up all hope." Wildenstein 1974, 1: 437.

15 Virginia Spate dates *The Meadow* to the following year based on stylistic grounds, while Wildenstein maintains that the painting was executed in 1879. *Poppy Field near Vétheuil* was one of six canvases sold to Mme. Cantin in November 1879. See Virginia Spate, *Claude Monet: His Life and Work* (New York, 1992), 143, n. 38 and Wildenstein 1996, 2: 209-210, W. 535.

16 Lionello Venturi, *Impressionists and Symbolists*, trans. Francis Steegmuller, (New York and London, 1950), 58.

17 "Ainsi Corot et Courbet ont franchi une partie de la distance qui séparait l'étude sur le terrain de la peinture du tableau, ils ont commencé à rendre les deux opérations, de successives, simultanées. Claude Monet, venu à son tour après eux, achève ce qu'ils avaient commencé. Avec lui, plus de croquis préliminaries accumulés, plus de crayons ou d'aquarelles utilisés à l'atelier, mais une peinture à l'huile tout entière commencée et terminée devant la scène naturelle, directement interprétée et rendue. Et c'est ainsi qu'il est devenu le chef de ce qu'à juste titre on a nommé 'l'école du plein air.'" Théodore Duret, preface to the catalogue of the exhibition at *La Vie Moderne*, quoted in *Critique d'avant-garde* (Paris, 1885), 96.

18 For a further discussion of the Taboureux interview with Monet for *La Vie Moderne*, see Annette Dixon's essay, pp. 101-102. Although Monet indicated to Taboureux that the view out his window was his "studio," it may be a misinterpretation of Monet's intent to assume that he was specifically telling Taboureux that he never worked indoors.

19 Lilla Cabot Perry, "Reminiscences of Claude Monet from 1889 to 1909," *The American Magazine of Art* 18, no. 3 (March 1927): 120.

20 John House and Robert L. Herbert have discussed Monet's working methods in detail. See House, *Monet: Nature into Art*, (New Haven and London, 1986) and Herbert, "Method and Meaning in Monet," *Art in America* 67 (September 1979): 90-108.

21 Joel Isaacson, "*La Débâcle* by Claude Monet," *Bulletin, Museums of Art and Archaeology, University of Michigan* 1 (1978), 4; Wildenstein 1974, 1:109.

22 An interesting corollary is Monet's decision not to varnish his paintings, a change that began in the 1880s. Michael Swicklik has proposed that this allowed Monet to continue to work on his paintings, possibly years after they were begun, until he was satisfied with their state of completion. See Michael Swicklik, "French Painting and the Use of Varnish, 1750-1900," *Studies in the History of Art: Conservation Research* (Washington, 1993), 157-174. My thanks to Kenneth Katz for bringing this article to my attention.

23 When challenged about the possible use of photographs employed in the studio-finishing of his series of London and Rouen Cathedral, Monet countered with the following: "... and whether my Cathedrals, my Londons and other canvases are painted from nature or not, that is nobody's business and is of no importance. I know so many painters who paint from nature and create nothing but horrors." Wildenstein 1985, 4:367, L. 1764, as quoted in House 1986, 151.

24 See Herbert 1994. For a further discussion of Monet's editing of the site, see also John House, "Time's Cycles," *Art in America* 80, no. 10 (October 1992): 126-135, 161.

25 Joel Isaacson, "Impressionism and Journalistic Illustration," *Arts Magazine* 56 (June, 1982): 95-115; Beatrice Farwell, *The Cult of Images*, exh. cat., The Art Museum, University of California, Santa Barbara, 1977; and Mark Roskill, "Early Impressionism and the Fashion Print," *Burlington Magazine* 112 (June 1970): 391-395.

For a discussion of the landscapists' relationship both to the landscape they portrayed and to the Paris art market, see John House, "Framing the Landscape," in *Impressions of France: Monet, Renoir, Pissarro, and their Rivals*, exh. cat., Hayward Gallery, London, and the Museum of Fine Arts, Boston, 1995-1996 (London and Boston, 1995).

26 It is also possible that Monet was playing down the prominence of the cliffs at Chantemesle. Downriver from Vétheuil rise a series of white outcroppings and caves. These white scars erupt from the otherwise green hills that extend in the direction of La Roche-Guyon and are clearly visible from the bank of the river at Vétheuil. Depending on where you stand along the bank, the outcroppings can be more or less intrusive in the landscape. In many of his views looking down the near branch of the Seine, Monet minimizes the sometimes harsh chromatic touches of the cliffs. This can be seen in two of the paintings in the present exhibition (pl. 3 and pl. 6). In the winter view of the hills the pale blue, mauve, and cool white hues allow the outcroppings to merge with the surrounding snow and ice; in the summer view of the same stretch of river Monet employs a looser brushwork to knit together the hills and the clouds. The same free handling of paint that shapes the hills and the outcroppings also piles up the wind-whipped clouds; in comparison to the upper portion of the painting, the surface of the river appears calm and placid.

27 It is interesting to compare the paintings of Vétheuil executed between 1878 and 1881 with the paintings of the town that he executed in the summer and early autumn of 1901 (W. 1635-1649). In these later paintings, his views from across the river at Lavacourt are painted from one vantage point and constitute a true series. Painted during afternoon visits to Lavacourt, to which Monet had traveled from Giverny in his new car, these works were now primarily explorations in the variations in color and light taken from one fixed point. His use of river traffic has changed. A few of the first paintings in the group include plants in the foreground of the near shore, as well as an occasional lone fishing boat. The references to the bank and the picturesque presence of the fishermen, which recall the paintings of Vétheuil from the 1870s and 1880s, are eliminated in the majority of the 1901 paintings. As a result, the 1901 paintings focus on the examination of afternoon color harmonies as Vétheuil is reflected in the Seine. There is one painting of this later series (W. 1647) in which a barge passing on the river has a prominent place in the composition. The barge along the river in this painting may also reflect a renewed familiarity with the paintings of Whistler, whose works he would have known from his recent trip to London. My thanks to Charles Stuckey for his helpful comments regarding the 1901 paintings. See Wildenstein 1996, 1:356-358, 4:734-742; Hoschedé 1960, 126-127; Paris, Réunion des musées nationaux, *Hommage à Claude Monet* (1840-1926), exh. cat. by Hélène Adhémar *et al.*, Grand Palais, 1980 (Paris, 1980), 308-311.

28 "Parmi ces peintres, au premier rang, je citerai Claude Monet. Celui-là a sucé le lait de notre âge, celui-là a grandi et grandira encore dans l'adoration de ce qui l'entoure. Il aime les horizons de nos villes, les taches grises et blanches que font les maisons sur le ciel clair; il aime, dans les rues, les gens qui courent, affairés, en paletots; il aime les champs de courses, les promenades aristocratiques où roule le tapage des voitures; il aime nos femmes, leur ombrelle, leurs gants, leurs chiffons, jusqu'à leurs faux cheveux et leur poudre de riz, tout ce qui les rend filles de notre civilisation.

"Dans les champs, Claude Monet préférera un parc anglais à un coin de forêt. Il se plaît à retrouver partout la trace de l'homme, il veut vivre toujours au milieu de nous. Comme un vrai Parisien, il emmène Paris à la campagne, il ne peut peindre un paysage sans y mettre des messieurs et des dames en toilette. La nature paraît perdre de son intérêt pour lui, dès qu'elle ne porte pas l'empreinte de nos mœurs." Emile Zola, "Les Actualistes," from *Mon Salon*, quoted in *Écrits sur l'art* (Paris, 1991), 207-208.

29 Brettell 1996, 101-102, argues that Monet's Seinescapes differ from Daubigny's quiet, rural views of the river. This is true of the paintings preceding the move to Vétheuil. The Argenteuil paintings include factories and other modern intrusions in the landscape along the Seine. However, although Monet's mode of depiction remains contemporary and modern, the views themselves do share a kinship with those of Daubigny.

30 See note 25 above.

31 The article by Georges Grison in *Le Figaro*, "La Débâcle de la Seine," lays out the history of severely cold winters in France. These hard freezes were followed by a rapid thaw and subsequent inundation. His chronicle went back as far as 1608, but compared the flood of 1830-1831, which older readers would still recall, with the present situation in Paris. He warned that a similar devastation could result once the ice melted, but reassured readers towards the end of the article that the government was taking all possible precautions to lessen the effects of the *débâcle* when it should begin, including dynamiting the ice to facilitate the movement of chunks of ice down the Seine; see Grison, "La Débâcle de la Seine," *Le Figaro* (December 31, 1879): 2. The periodical *La Nature* also chronicled the history of severe cold and winter floods, reporting on legendary winters as far back as the year 544. The winter of 1812 was also considered exceptionally severe with the lowest temperature ever recorded in France to that date: minus 31 degrees (Celsius). The author remarked that the severe winter of 1870-1871 had contributed to the suffering of Parisians during the Franco-Prussian war: "Cependant personne n'oubliera l'hiver 1870-1871, où pendant la terrible invasion prussienne, la rigueur des gelées semblait ajouter à la liste de nos ennemis." See Gaston Tissandier, "Les Grands froids à propos de l'hiver 1879-80," *La Nature*, premier semestre (January-June, 1880): 56-59. *Le Monde illustré* also provided an extended

account of the breakup of the ice. See "La Débâcle de la Seine," vol. 24, no. 1189, (January 10, 1880): 22-23.

32 This low reading was recorded by officals at the parc de Saint-Maur at 1:00 a.m. on December 10. See "Nos Gravures, l'hiver à Paris," *L'Illustration* 24, no. 1921 (December 20, 1879): 390.

33 Heavy snow fell on December 5, with enough accumulation of snow (25-30 cm) that by noon trams could not get through and circulation within Paris was impeded. "Nouvelles Diverses," *Le Figaro* (December 5, 1879): 2. Detailing the difficulty in navigating around the city, one writer for *L'Illustration* noted that pedestrians and coaches found moving nearly impossible, and omnibuses required three, four, or even five horses to pull in the snow, "Nos Gravures," *L'Illustration* 24, no. 1921 (December 20, 1879): 390.

Downriver at Vétheuil, the snowfall of early December made passage between the train station at Mantes-la-Jolie and Vétheuil impassable. When Ernest Hoschedé was returning to Vétheuil several days later, on December 8, the twelve-kilometer trip still took three hours. See Wildenstein 1996, 1:150

34 "L'hiver à Paris," *L'Illustration* 25, no. 1923 (January 3, 1880): 7.

35 "Nouvelles Diverses," *Le Figaro* (December 24, 1879): 3.

36 "Nouvelles Diverses," *Le Figaro* (December 13, 1879): 2.

37 "Les traîneaux et le patinage à Paris," *La Nature*, premier semestre (January-June, 1880): 78. The Christmas celebrations included skating at nighttime with Venetian lanterns, "Faits-Paris," *Le Voltaire* (December 25, 1879): 2.

38 ". . . le froid a repris de plus belle, et Paris c'est réveillé de nouveau en grelottant. Une givre épais avait recouvert jusqu'aux plus petites brindilles des branches d'arbre, et l'effet produit par cette métamorphose était fort curieux. Ainsi parés, les arbres ressemblaient à de gigantesques panaches de plumes blanches." "Nouvelles Diverses," *Le Figaro* (December 15, 1879): 2.

39 "La Buvette groënlandaise du quai d'Hôtel-de-Ville," *Le Monde illustré* 23, no. 1187 (December 27, 1879), 411.

40 "Nouvelles Diverses," *Le Figaro* (December 31, 1879): 4.

41 "Nouvelles Diverses," *Le Figaro* (December 30, 1879): 2; "Nouvelles Diverses," *Le Figaro* (December 31, 1879): 4; Georges Grison, "La Débâcle de la Seine," *Le Figaro* (December 31, 1879): 2; "Nouvelles Diverses," *Le Figaro* (January 1, 1880): 2.

42 Gaston Tissandier, "La Débâcle de la Seine (le 3 janvier 1880)," *La Nature*, premier semestre (January-June, 1880): 116-118.

43 See articles in *Le Figaro*, "Nouvelles Diverses," (January 3, 1880): 3; "Nouvelles Diverses," (January 4, 1880): 2; and "Nouvelles Diverses," (January 5, 1880): 2.

44 See "Nos Gravures," *L'Illustration* 25, no. 1924 (January 10, 1880): 27, and "La Débâcle," *Le Figaro* (January 5, 1880): 2.

45 *L'Illustration* 24, no. 1921 (December 20, 1879): 390; *Le Monde illustré* 23, no. 1185 (December 13, 1879): 378; *Le Monde illustré* 23, no. 1186 (December 20, 1879): 394.

46 "Nouvelles Diverses," *Le Figaro* (January 4, 1880): 2; "Nos Gravures," *L'Illustration* 25, no. 1924 (January 10, 1880): 27; "Courrier de Paris," *L'Illustration* 25, no. 1924 (January 10, 1880): 22.

47 Wildenstein 1996, 1: 148-154 recounts the period of the freezing of the Seine and subsequent breakup of the ice. See 151.

48 *Ibid.*, 1:152-153, and Wildenstein 1991, 5:438, L.170.

49 *Ibid.*, 1:151-152 and *passim.*

50 *Ibid.*, 1:152.

51 *Ibid.*

52 *Ibid.*

53 See Isaacson 1978, 5-6.

54 According to Wildenstein, W. 557 contained two figures which were still visible in the painting in 1905, after which they were overpainted. See Wildenstein 1996, 2: 217.

55 G. de Cherville, in his article "Lettres de mon jardin," may have most aptly summed up the feeling that the harsh winter might have evoked in a fellow-gardener like Monet when, writing in December before the thaw, he speaks of "this terror of the snow" and its effect on plants and wildlife. "Tout cela est d'autant plus grandiose que l'invasion a été plus brusque, et cependant, même avec l'appoint de ce soleil d'hiver qui illumine sans réchauffer, je ne crois pas possible de contempler ce paysage sans un profond serrement de cœur," *L'Illustration* 24, no. 1921 (December 20, 1879): 394-395.

56 Grace Seiberling, *Monet's Series*, Ph.D. diss., Yale University, 1976 (New York and London, 1981), 49-55.

Annette Dixon

The Marketing of Monet: The Exhibition at *La Vie Moderne*

Introduction: Rejection and Reaction

In April 1880 the news reached Monet and his circle that of the two paintings he had submitted to the Salon that year, only one canvas would be shown. We do not know the reasons the jury accepted *La Seine à Lavacourt*[1] (*The Seine at Lavacourt*, W. 578,[2] pl. 7, hereafter simply *Lavacourt*) yet refused *Les Glaçons* (*The Ice Floes*, W. 568, fig. 1).[3] Émile Zola's comment that *Lavacourt* had been received only "out of charity"[4] seems to imply that even the accepted painting had trouble getting into the Salon. If Monet's own description of *Les Glaçons* as "one of my good things" two years later[5] is any indication of his feelings about that work in April 1880, it is likely that the refusal of this painting was a blow to him. In response to this semi-rejection, his friends rallied around him, organizing a one-man exhibition for him at the gallery of the journal *La Vie Moderne*. This show, which featured the rejected Salon submission *Les Glaçons*, was to turn Monet's life around.

A sort of small retrospective, the exhibition focused on works that Monet had recently painted at Vétheuil. Two of the works in the show, one of them *Les Glaçons*, gave Monet a way to make public the fresh direction that his art had taken with his *Débâcles*, a series of eighteen stark and haunting scenes of the ice-choked Seine, painted following the thawing of the frozen river. This painting campaign came in the midst of intense difficulties. Some were personal: cohabitation, under financial duress, of the families of Monet and his friend and patron Ernest Hoschedé in the fall of 1878; and the loss of his wife Camille in September 1879. Others were professional: critics had

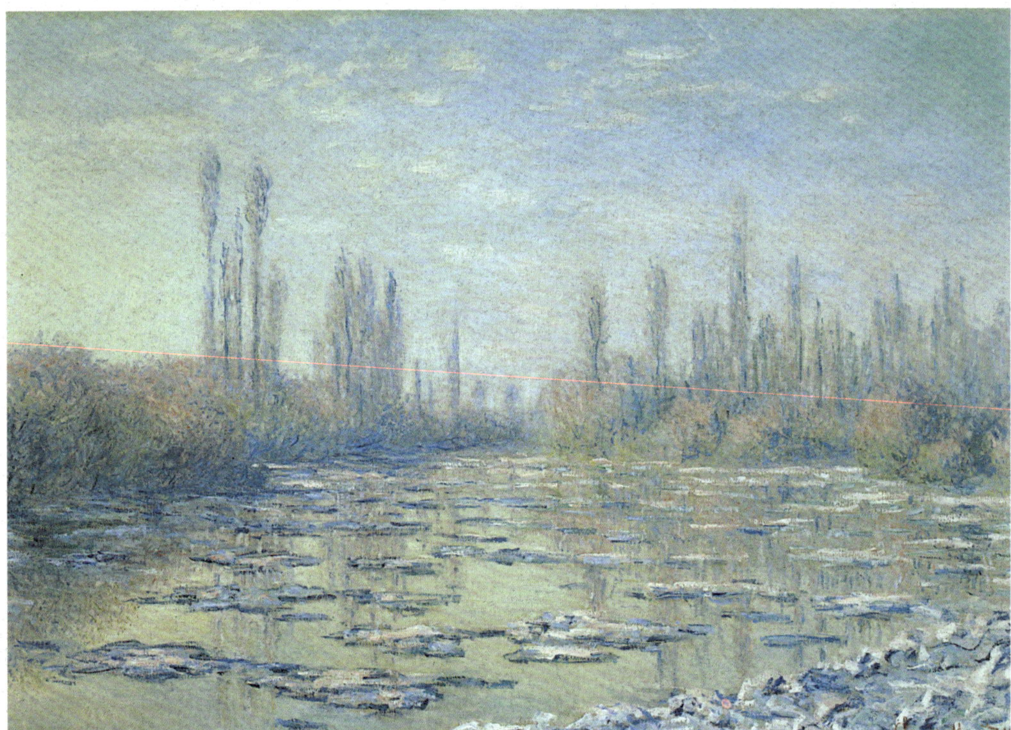

Fig. 1
Claude Monet
Les Glaçons
(The Ice Floes)
1880
Oil on canvas
W. 568
Shelburne Museum, Shelburne, Vermont (27.1.2-108)

castigated Monet's sketchy manner of painting in their reviews of the Impressionist exhibition of 1879, and his landscape paintings proved virtually unmarketable that fall. The *Vie Moderne* show created renewed interest in Monet on the part of critics and collectors.

The publications associated with the show—an interview in the journal by reporter Émile Taboureux[6] and an introduction to the catalogue of the exhibition by Monet's friend the avant-garde critic Théodore Duret[7]—were informed by a myth concerning his *plein-air* painting methods, namely that Monet worked entirely outdoors and not in the studio at all.[8] But we know from his letters that Monet often finished open-air paintings in his atelier; in his small house at Vétheuil, his bedroom, the attic, or the sheltered courtyard may have served as a work space.[9] Furthermore, various groups of works that Monet executed in the 1870s include small sketches done on the spot as well as larger, or more finished, works done in the studio. For example, two of the four views of the Tuileries garden that Monet painted from Victor Chocquet's apartment in 1876 were sketches (W. 403-404), while the two others were studio pictures (W. 401-402);[10] two of the decorative panels that Monet executed at Montgeron for the Hoschedés in 1876 (W. 418, W. 420) were preceded by studies (W. 417, W. 419);[11] and of the twelve canvases in the Gare Saint-Lazare series of 1877, two were much larger paintings than the others (W. 438-439).[12] Recent Monet studies have asserted that Monet himself took an active hand in propagating the myth that he painted only out-of-doors.[13] However, it is far from clear that Monet was trying to manipulate what was said about him in 1880. The few remarks of Monet's that are preserved from this time—some found in his correspondence and others reported in Taboureux's article—need to be reexamined. The present essay takes a close look at these and at the strategies that Monet's admirers developed to create a market for his work through the vehicle of the one-man show and its accompanying publications.

The essay also examines in some detail the particulars of this turning point in Monet's career. How did the exhibition come about at all? While Monet himself may not had have enough clout with *La Vie Moderne* publisher Georges Charpentier to approach him for an exhibition, some of his friends—Pierre Auguste Renoir, Édouard Manet, Duret, and Hoschedé—did. It was very likely one or more of them who persuaded the publisher to give Monet a solo show, as I will discuss below. Exhibitions in intimate settings focusing on the work of a single artist were quite new when Charpentier's newspaper started holding them on its premises in 1879 (and such one-artist shows remained unusual even in the 1890s when they became Monet's preferred mode of presentation for his series paintings).[14] At the *Vie Moderne* show the rejected *Glaçons* became something of a badge of honor by virtue of being listed first in the catalogue. *Les Glaçons* elicited praise in the press in 1880 and again in 1882, reversing a tide of negative criticism against Monet's sketchiness that had crested with the fourth Impressionist exhibition of 1879.[15] The painting, desired by at least two other collectors (Ratisbonne and Ephrussi[16]), was bought at a handsome price by Charpentier's wife as a present for her husband after he had much admired it. This purchase, as well as others from the show and from works in Monet's stock, stimulated a quantum leap in the prices that Monet's paintings fetched, even compared to the price that dealer Georges Petit paid him for a still-life painting a few months before. The financial tide had turned in Monet's favor.

Monet and the Salon of 1880

Monet had many reasons to enter the Salon in 1880. Having come to feel that the Impressionist group shows depressed his and his colleagues' sales,[17] Monet at first planned not to join the group exhibition in 1879, but was persuaded to by Gustave Caillebotte, who assembled the works for him.[18] The scathing criticism of his works in the fourth Impressionist show (most of them scenes he had made recently at Vétheuil) may have been among the factors that prompted him to seek another exhibition mode. Remarks by the most influential Parisian art critic of the moment, Albert Wolff, and by novelist and critic Zola, reflected the controversy over the degree of finish necessary for a painting to be considered complete—a *tableau*, rather than a sketch, a study, or a fragmentary version (*esquisse, pochade, ébauche, étude, morceau*).[19] Wolff upbraided Monet for making "impulsive sketches" (*pochades primesautières*) and for having sent "thirty landscapes that seemed to have been done in an afternoon."[20] Zola, while acknowledging that Monet rendered nature faithfully, nevertheless condemned the artist for producing paintings hastily, for being satisfied with "the approximate," and for not studying nature "with the passion of real creators."[21] Armand Silvestre took a different tack; while this reviewer praised Monet's views of flags marking the June 30 holiday of 1878 for their "verve and audacity," other entries, including some of his Vétheuil paintings, "were, to tell the truth, predictable and do not give any new direction."[22] Monet may have found Silvestre's criticism especially stinging since among that reviewer's long-standing writings on Monet, his preface to the albums of etchings of works in the Durand-Ruel gallery's holdings of 1873 had singled Monet out as the boldest Impressionist painter.[23] In their strange beauty, Monet's *Débâcle* paintings might have been to some degree inspired by Silvestre's opinion that the artist had been continuing with the same old approach for too long.

Wolff had sarcastically noted that "as soon as one of them [the Impressionists] makes an almost proper painting, which has some chance of being accepted at the Salon, he deserts the others," a remark that might have prompted Monet, already frustrated with the group shows, to consider submitting to the Salon.[24] Renoir had done just that before the Salon of 1879 and succeeded. This must have offered Monet hope, even though the last time he had been received by the Salon had been in 1868. Monet must have been heartened by recent governmental reforms in the category of landscape, both in the admission of landscape artists to the jury and the provision for first-class medals, as well as the invitation extended by the new minister of fine arts Jules Ferry to *plein-air* painters to submit landscapes to the Salon of 1880.[25]

Further encouragement was offered by one of Monet's collectors, Duret. The latter wrote frequently to several of the Impressionists, urging them to show at the Salon, where they were more likely to reach a large public.[26] Monet's letter of March 8, 1880 to Duret refers to such counsel: "Because you are among those who have often advised me to expose myself again to the judgment of the official jury, I must let you know that I am going to attempt this test." Yet Monet regarded entering the Salon with some distaste. As he said in the same letter to Duret, ". . . it is not by inclination that

I do this, and it is really unfortunate that the press and the public took so little seriously our little exhibitions much preferable to this official bazaar."[27]

Yet perhaps the decisive factor in persuading Monet to enter the Salon was Petit's purchase in December 1879 of a still life of a basket of fruit, *Corbeille de fruits*, probably W. 545, now at the Metropolitan Museum of Art (pl. 11), for 500 francs—a higher price than the artist normally received—along with two snow landscapes (unidentified) for 300 francs together. Petit promised further purchases if Monet stopped selling for low prices[28] and if Monet entered the Salon.[29] As Wildenstein notes, Petit did not wait for Monet to enter the Salon; in February 1880, he bought a painting of pheasants, possibly W. 549, painted between December 1879 and January 1880.[30] By that time there had already been rumors that Monet would enter the Salon, as suggested by an anonymous and venomous notice that appeared in January in the journal *Le Gaulois*, an organ generally sympathetic to the Impressionists.[31] Signed "Tout Paris," this article rhetorically announced the death of Monet. His fellow artists Degas, Rafaëlli, Cassatt, Caillebotte, Pissarro, Forain, Braquemond, and Rouart were said to have invited the public not to attend his funeral, which would be held in the Salon of Cabanel on May 1. In addition, the article made insinuating comments about Monet's living arrangement with Alice Hoschedé (whom it apparently meant when referring to Monet's "wife") and her husband Ernest, who, it alleged, was living off of Monet.

Monet reacted by writing a letter of protest to *Le Gaulois*.[32] He suspected collector Georges de Bellio[33] as well as Pissarro, conveying to the latter his suspicions of all his Impressionist friends.[34] On March 8, 1880 Monet wrote to Duret that he was being treated by the Impressionists as a traitor.[35] Degas called Monet's desertion a "frantic publicity stunt" (*réclame effrénée*). We know of Degas' remark (apparently contained in a letter, now lost?) only from Venturi: "[Monet's] half-success at the Salon of 1880 exposes him to the criticisms of Zola and to the anger of Degas, who rails against Monet's 'frantic publicity stunt.'" Venturi's brief reference to Degas' remark seems to involve only Monet's partial success at the Salon, rather than the show at the *Vie Moderne* as well, contrary to one recent assertion.[36]

SALON SUBMISSIONS AND RESULTS

Monet's letter to Duret informed the critic that he was at work on three large paintings, though only two were for the Salon. One Monet judged too much to his own taste to send (most likely the very sketchy *Soleil couchant sur la Seine, effet d'hiver (Sunset on the Seine, Winter Effect*, W. 576, Musée du Petit Palais, fig. 2), concluding that it would surely be refused. In its place he was doing "something more discreet, more

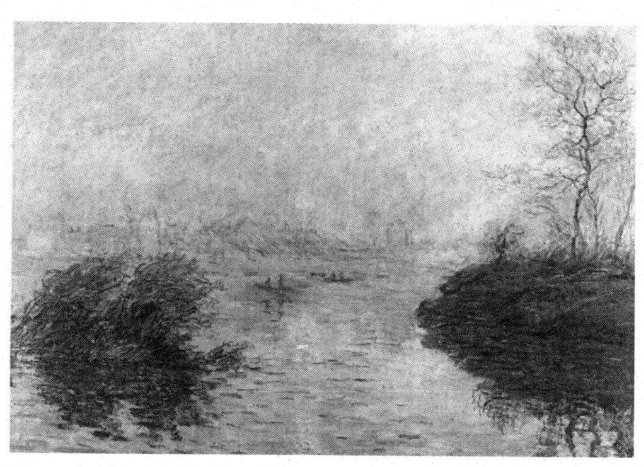

Fig. 2
Claude Monet
Soleil couchant sur la Seine, effet d'hiver
(Sunset on the Seine, Winter Effect)
1880
Oil on canvas
W. 576
Musée du Petit Palais, Paris

bourgeois" (*une chose plus sage, plus bourgeoise*). Scholars disagree as to whether this painting was *Lavacourt* or *Les Glaçons*,[37] for nowhere did Monet indicate which painting he meant. *Lavacourt* has suffered in its reputation for having been accepted by the Salon, and thus has often been seen as the more conventional of the two; even at the start *Les Glaçons* fared better for having been rejected, and hence has often been considered the more daring of the two.[38]

Lavacourt depicts the village of the same name on the island-studded Seine across from Vétheuil, with a church steeple on a hilltop in the distance; the scene is awash with morning light. *Les Glaçons* is a glowing, rosy sunset scene showing ice floes melting with no hint of human presence. The two works derive from different strains of Barbizon or Pre-Impressionist painting: *Lavacourt* recalls Daubigny in its depiction of a river landscape that includes references to human culture and that concerns itself closely with light values; *Les Glaçons* harks back to Rousseau in its depiction of water edged with symmetrically arranged trees and its exclusion of all but nature. Both works combine these traditional features with more startling aspects: the predominantly pale blue coloration of *Lavacourt*, which gives the work a strong sense of light and atmosphere;[39] the loose brushwork of *Les Glaçons*, which stresses the picture surface,[40] and the latter painting's "decorative and artificial" arrangement of pastel colors.[41] Perhaps it was not on the basis of conventionality or unconventionality that one of Monet's paintings was accepted by the Salon and one rejected. The reason may have been purely practical: one wonders whether the jury had only one prize to allot to Monet.

Unlike *Les Glaçons*, which was praised in the press immediately upon being exhibited at *La Vie Moderne*, *Lavacourt* was barely mentioned by reviewers. They noted the painting's luminosity, but also remarked on its unfortunate placement on the wall. Both Monet's and Renoir's paintings had been hung so high that they could barely be seen. Using Cézanne as a go-between, Monet and Renoir asked Zola to take up their cause in the press.[42] A series of articles in *Le Voltaire* criticizing both the Salon and the Impressionists resulted.[43] Zola noted that Monet's painting had been poorly placed.[44]

Briefly describing the painting, he extolled its exquisite note of light and the outdoors amid the dark paintings around it. He went on to describe Monet as "an incomparable landscapist" but then said that he had put out too many sketches. He advised Monet to devote himself to important paintings, worked up after long study, implying that *Lavacourt* was not an important painting.[45] Yet, as Levine has pointed out, this was a large painting four times the size of most Impressionist canvases and apparently done in the studio from on-the-site sketches.[46] Zola may not have known that Monet did work up *Lavacourt* from several sketches.[47] Zola's back-handed support for *Lavacourt* was in marked contrast to critics' eventual reactions to the painting that was refused by the Salon, *Les Glaçons*.

Philippe de Chennevières, director of the Fine Arts administration, writing in the *Gazette des Beaux-Arts*, pointed out that Monet's painting was "lost in the friezes of one of the rooms." He added that seeing it more closely would not help, because its "luminous and clear atmosphere makes all the nearby landscapes in the same gallery seem 'black.'"[48] The pale hues and sharp contrasts of value in *Lavacourt* clearly did not accord with official taste.[49] Philippe Burty noted in *L'Art* that because of the poor placement of Monet's painting "all the delicacy of his palette evaporates with no benefit for him, or for the public, which was starting to develop a taste for his subtle indications." He asserted that landscapes in the Salon, presumably including Monet's, had lost the notion of the *tableau*, or fully accomplished painting, implying that they remained at the level of sketches or preparatory works.[50] But writing in *La République Française*, Burty advised his readers to view Monet not at the Salon, where "all the fresh qualities of his Lavacourt evaporate," but at his one-man show at *La Vie Moderne*, where they could admire his rejected painting the *Débâcle* (i.e., *Les Glaçons*).[51] Even Monet's successful entry at the Salon was plainly a painting in search of its proper venue.

THE EXHIBITION IN THE OFFICES OF *LA VIE MODERNE*

Having an exhibition sponsored by *La Vie Moderne* put Monet in the spotlight, and brought him to the attention of the readers of the fashionable new journal as well as the elite who attended the parties given by the wife of its publisher. The publicity campaign organized by the journal—interview, exhibition review, and the introduction to the exhibition catalogue—served Monet's friends in the cause of promoting the artist. This campaign was a step up from the treatment accorded Renoir and Manet in their one-man shows at *La Vie Moderne*. Renoir's exhibition had been accompanied by a review by his own brother.[52] Manet's had been accompanied by an exhibition catalogue listing the paintings (but apparently without an essay) and a review.[53] Neither Renoir nor Manet seems to have had an interview.

The weekly was established in April 1879 by Georges Charpentier, who had published such naturalist authors as Zola, the Goncourts, Maupassant, and Daudet. The publisher founded it at the urging of his wife, who ran the most celebrated salon in Paris. Her guests included luminaries from many fields, such as the aforementioned authors, the painters Manet and Renoir, the critics Duret and Huysmans, and the politicians Gambetta and Clemenceau.[54] (The last-named, with his writings on Monet, was also to help perpetuate elements of Monet's legend.) *La Vie Moderne* was "devoted to artistic, literary and worldly life,"[55] though with hardly any mention of politics (except for Gambetta).[56] It also included articles aimed at women, reflecting the interests of Madame Charpentier.[57] Designed to appeal to the upper bourgeois class, the magazine was not radical, but rather promoted what was new, the very essence of modernity, as its title suggested.[58] Armand Silvestre, writing in the first issue, stressed the journal's focus on the fashions of the moment: "Modern life" (*la vie moderne*) "is achieved today in the sincerity of its allures, its manner and its dress."[59] Rather than formulate taste, the journal sought to popularize it and seek a middle ground between what was current taste and what was more avant-garde.[60] Its illustrations included reproductions of drawings by Bonnat and Gérôme alongside those by Degas and Cassatt.[61]

La Vie Moderne housed in its offices a gallery in which it featured the work of contemporary artists. Edmond Renoir, the younger brother of the artist, and at that time editor-in-chief of *La Presse*, was put in charge of exhibitions.[62] In the first issue Edmond felt compelled to explain the nature of the series of exhibitions that the gallery intended to organize, as the one-man format at that time was still unusual.[63] These small shows, scheduled at "close intervals," would allow the public to get to know the works of one artist at a time in an intimate and concentrated way. He stressed that these exhibitions would be "nothing else than the studio of the artist transported momentarily to the boulevard, in a gallery accessible to everyone."[64] Indeed, although the gallery itself was small and poorly lit, the location of the newspaper's rented offices encouraged passers-by. The offices were in a wine shop on the boulevard des Italiens, at the entrance of the Passage du Prince.[65]

The first one-person shows in the gallery were of artists outside the Impressionist circle: Ulysse Butin, Giuseppe (Joseph) de Nittis, Louise Abbema, and Antoine Vollon.[66] However, in June 1879, on the heels of his Salon success, Renoir had his first one-man show there; the exhibition featured pastels.[67] In April 1880 Manet was given a solo show, comprised of oils and pastels, after having participated with other artists in more whimsical shows of painted tambourines and ostrich eggs decorated for Easter.[68] It was in this gallery that mixed non-Impressionists with Impressionists, popular objects with serious works, that Monet's first one-artist show was held, providing the first venue for the showing of the rejected Salon work, other *Débâcles*, and works created at Vétheuil.

There is a mystery as to how—not long after the news came out in April 1880 that *Les Glaçons* had been rejected by the Salon jury—an exhibition was arranged for Monet in the gallery of *La Vie Moderne*, a one-man show that would showcase the rejected *Glaçons* and works that he had recently produced at Vétheuil. In a letter that I will discuss in more detail below, Monet expressed to his friend Duret mixed feelings about the usefulness of this exhibition,[69] which suggests that Monet did not initiate the idea of the show. Who approached publisher Charpentier? Monet's relationship to Charpentier makes it unlikely that it was he who came to the publisher with the idea. While Charpentier had been a supporter of Monet's in the mid-1870s, the artist's wooing of this patron had more recently been only moderately successful.

Charpentier had been a Monet collector since 1876; three *pochades*, or rapid sketches, are recorded in Monet's account book for May 1876, and three *toiles*, or canvases, are recorded for January 1877.[70] One of these was *Le Port du Havre, effet de nuit* (*The Port of Le Havre, Night Effect*, W. 264), a dark variant of *Impression, soleil levant* (*Impression, Sunrise*, W. 263), attesting to this patron's interest in Monet's sketchy compositions. According to some of Monet's letters of 1876, Monet had hoped Charpentier would buy his *Train dans la neige, la locomotive* (*The Train Engine in the Snow*, W. 365) which eventually went to de Bellio.[71] One Monet painting from Charpentier's collection, a painting of a basket of flowers, was included in the Impressionist group exhibition in 1877.[72] From 1877 to 1878, Monet sometimes asked Charpentier for money, at least once offering to reimburse him either in paintings or in money; but the publisher acquired nothing from the artist after the group of purchases in January 1877.[73] From late 1878 until the *Vie Moderne* show, Charpentier's interest in Monet's work seems to have fluctuated. In mid-December 1878, following up on indications that Charpentier had given him about his interest in buying, Monet deposited with that patron a painting that he thought Charpentier would like: Monet asked for 140 francs but wrote that 100 francs would be all right.[74] However, in late January 1879, Charpentier had not responded at all to Monet's offer.[75] In October of that year Monet asked Charpentier to come to his Paris flat to see some new works that he had brought from Vétheuil.[76] But Charpentier's interest deepened only on the occasion of Monet's show at *La Vie Moderne*, at which the collector found the rejected Salon painting particularly intriguing. Someone besides Monet, a real insider in the Charpentier circle with influence on him, is more likely to have persuaded Charpentier to show the artist's works.

As a frequent visitor to Madame Charpentier's Salon[77] and as her favorite artist, Renoir is one strong candidate; the portrait of Madame Charpentier and her daughters (now at the Metropolitan Museum of Art), commissioned from Renoir in 1878, had had a great triumph at the Salon of 1879. As noted above, it was Renoir's brother Edmond who was in charge of the series of exhibitions in the *Vie Moderne* gallery. Furthermore, promoting the showing of a rejected Salon work in the gallery was something that Renoir had already tried. At the time of his own one-man show at *La Vie Moderne* in June 1879, he was able to get the gallery to agree to mount a show for Sisley, who had been rejected by the Salon of 1879. However, Sisley's show was postponed until 1881.[78]

Manet also might have approached Charpentier. Early in April 1880 Manet had received a letter from Antoine Guillemet, who sat on the Salon jury, and who probably learned that Monet had been partially rejected and then told his friends.[79] Manet had been a longtime supporter of Monet, often lending him money or making purchases.[80] That Manet himself was having a show that very month in the *Vie Moderne* gallery may indicate that he was in a favored position in the Charpentier circle. However, according to Tabarant, Manet seems to have been surprised by getting a one-man show—the journal had not seemed in a hurry to organize one for him, although he had had entries in shows of decorated tambourines and Easter eggs.[81] Another thing suggests that Manet may have had some influence in getting Monet his show: Manet did a sketch portraying Monet that appeared both in Taboureux's interview in the journal and in Duret's introductory essay for the catalogue for the show.

As I will discuss below, two other friends of Monet who were habitués of Madame Charpentier's salon served as organizers of the show—the critic Duret and Monet's colleague Hoschedé.[82] Léger assumed that these organizers persuaded the journal to give an exhibition to Monet.[83] While their collaboration with Monet on the show might speak for them as candidates, the evidence for either Renoir or Manet seems just as compelling. While we may never know who was responsible for securing Charpentier's agreement to a show for Monet, the most important point is that these people were in a position to create an opportunity for Monet with a new sort of exhibition mode, and constituted a group who, as artists or collectors, had a vested interest in seeing Monet's career and the cause of Impressionism furthered.[84] Monet had little need to be manipulative about his own reputation with all this potential help from powerful friends at hand.

While Duret and Hoschedé organized the logistics of the show, Monet himself was involved as well. The first that we know of the planning of a show for Monet is a letter that he wrote to *La Vie Moderne* director Émile Bergerat in April 1880 asking for details on the exhibition. At this point the show and the accompanying article were planned for May.[85] However, the show was postponed until June, presumably because of Monet's own self-questioning. A letter written to Duret just over two weeks before the opening of the show on June 7 hints at the painter's ambivalence. He says that he is completely discouraged, and were it not for the involvement of Duret and Hoschedé at *La Vie Moderne*, he would renounce the show, for which he sees neither the interest nor the usefulness. He confesses that he has nothing new to put in it. He has been working but does not have anything worth showing.[86] This letter echoes earlier complaints; Monet had shown a similar moodiness and lack of self-confidence concerning the Impressionist group show of 1879 as well as the Salon of 1880, in both cases managing to pull something together.[87]

Monet actively participated with Duret, and apparently also with Hoschedé,[88] in the organization of the catalogue, as well as the hanging and opening of the show (presumably a private reception on the evening before the public opening on June 7).[89] Monet worked with Duret on getting loans from various people for the show: Caillebotte sent a painting,[90] and two came from Theulier, one depicting the aftermath of the *débâcle* and the other a still life.[91] Monet made sure to have the paintings and frames (presumably for the show) picked up.[92] In a letter to Duret written on July 5, 1880 Monet expresses his gratitude to his friend for his collaboration on the show and says he is working on a painting as a means of thanking him.[93]

The Marketing of Monet

The two publications that *La Vie Moderne* commissioned to accompany the show played important roles in the marketing of the artist. These were the interview by the reporter Taboureux in April, which appeared as an article in June, and Duret's introductory essay to the catalogue.[94] Commissioning Duret to write the introduction to the catalogue reflected the late nineteenth-century trend of trying to add prestige to an exhibition catalogue by including an art historian's introduction.[95] Both publications promoted the story that Monet painted entirely out-of-doors. Taboureux's interview in *La Vie Moderne* was the basis for the *plein-air* legend, today regarded as partly Monet's creation. It was to be recounted over the course of Monet's life. But Monet's active involvement may have been minimal in 1880.[96]

In his article Taboureux noted that he met Monet on his "port"—several planks hammered together, edged with a primitive balustrade. Responding to Taboureux's request to take him to his studio, Monet replied: "'My studio! But I have never had a studio and I do not understand shutting oneself up in a room. To draw, yes; to paint, no.' And with a gesture as broad as the horizon, pointing to the Seine all strewn with the gold of the setting sun, to the hills bathed in cool shadows, and to all of Vétheuil that seemed to sleep in the quiet of the April sun . . . : 'Here's my studio, mine!'"[97] On the surface, the ingredients of the legend are here. Yet Monet's statement is puzzling. How well could it have served his cause, given that Zola and Wolff had criticized him in 1879 for doing half-finished, hasty work? The implication was that Monet did not spend enough time in the studio. Furthermore, Monet may have had a practical reason for saying he did not have an indoor studio. During the course of the interview the two paid a visit to Monet's house; Taboureux makes no mention of a studio there. It may be that Monet simply did not show it to him for reasons of privacy. Since his studio was in the bedroom or attic in a house with Alice and the children, he probably did not want to reveal that to the world, especially since there had been hints of impropriety in his living arrangement in the article in *Le Gaulois*.[98]

When Taboureux remarked on his absence from the Impressionist show that year, Monet said: ". . . I am always and I want always to be an Impressionist. . . but I see my colleagues, men and women, only rarely. The little church has become today a banal school that opens its doors to the first dauber to come." (*La petite église est devenue aujourd'hui une école banale qui ouvre ses portes au premier barbouilleur venu.*)[99] Monet scored several rhetorical points with this remark. On the one hand, he could refute the rumors, published previously in *Le Gaulois*, that he was deserting the Impressionists,[100] and continue to claim the mantle of Impressionism for himself. On the other hand, he could criticize the Impressionists for allowing into their ranks a newcomer, such as Rafaëlli or Gauguin, to replace him.[101] Monet, who had organized earlier Impressionist shows, but had indeed left the group, showed a clever kind of diplomacy.

When the reporter asked Monet to give him more details on his work as a painter, Monet treated him rather rudely, thrusting into his hand a bundle of newspapers with his reviews instead of answering questions about his manner of working. This indicates clearly that, whatever the efforts expended by his friends, Monet did not enjoy this interview. The reporter was severely insulted. He wrote in the article that after the interview he brought the documents with him to his hotel, wrote his article, and went to bed without reading them. He resolved to return "the very interesting newspapers" to Monet the next morning "without having read a darned line" (*sans en avoir lu une traitre ligne*). He ended the article by asking Monet sarcastically, "This is how we usually treat our friends, isn't it, Monet?"[102] To be sure, the myth of Monet as a painter submerged in nature makes an appearance in Taboureux's piece, but Monet's own interest level was low.

It fell to Duret to go into more detail about Monet's working method,[103] situating Monet in an art-historical lineage. Duret's essay specifically aimed to counter the negative criticism concerning hasty execution that Monet had received in 1879 and 1880.[104] His strategy was to establish how Monet's method of creating a painting was distinct from that of his predecessors and carried its own advantages. Duret described Rousseau's more deliberate manner of working up a painting from many outdoor sketches and studies, based on which he composed a *tableau* after returning to the studio. He then described how Corot and Courbet went beyond Rousseau and collapsed these distinct phases of work, painting outdoors directly in oil and finishing these studies in the studio to make a *tableau*, or using them as the basis for more developed, larger *tableaux*.[105]

Duret asserted that Monet went further still. He made simultaneous what was separate in the practice of the earlier artists, refraining from making a set of preliminary sketches, completely beginning and finishing an oil painting entirely in front of the natural scene, which he directly interpreted and rendered.[106] Working outdoors in all seasons, the painter's habit, Duret wrote, was to cover a white canvas suddenly with marks of color corresponding to colored spots of the scene that he observed. Since often he could only get a sketch in the first sitting, the next day he came back and added to the first sketch, accenting details and firming up contours; he continued until he was satisfied.[107] Duret then pointed out the advantages of painting on the spot: it enabled Monet to notice and render fugitive effects neglected by his predecessors—"the most ephemeral and the most delicate" aspects of light, air, and atmosphere.[108]

Duret's comments fly in the face of what we know about Monet's work not only on *Lavacourt* and on *Les Glaçons*, but also on most of the other paintings in the *Débâcle* series. Monet had based the two large paintings that he had submitted to the Salon on earlier sketches—W. 475 and W. 538-540 in the case of *Lavacourt*,[109] and W. 567 in the case of *Les Glaçons*.[110] Monet's letter to Duret in March informing him that he was working on paintings for the Salon thus implied work in the atelier.[111] As for the works in the *Débâcle* series, Monet probably could not have finished all of them in front of the motif. Wildenstein points to the limited number of daylight hours available;[112] there are also the factors of the bitter cold, which would have impeded work, as well as the thawing of the ice, which sometimes melted fast. It is thus likely that

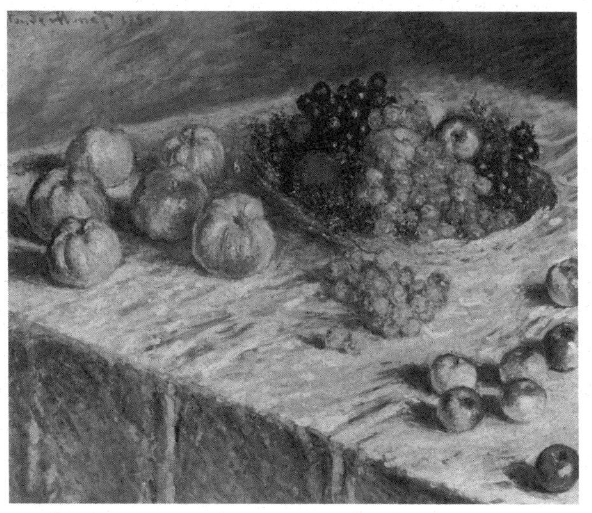

Fig. 3
Claude Monet
Nature morte: pommes et raisin
(Still Life: Apples and Grapes)
1880
Oil on canvas
W. 546
The Art Institute of Chicago, Mr. and Mrs. Martin A. Ryerson Collection, 1933.1152.

only a few of the *Débâcle* paintings were done completely *in situ*—the rest were probably worked up in the atelier. Monet even wrote to Duret in January about the sudden thawing of the Seine and said that he had tried to make a painting of the thawing ice, but that it had melted so quickly that he could only make a sketch instead.[113]

Clearly, Duret was aware that Monet made both sketches and finished paintings. Furthermore, it is not just Monet's studio at Vétheuil that Duret did not report; during the Vétheuil period Monet also kept a studio in Paris on the rue Vintimille, as numerous letters of his attest. While Duret and Monet may indeed have talked about his working method, it seems unlikely that Monet would have contributed to falsifying the record about how he made paintings.[114]

THE WORKS IN THE EXHIBITION

At *La Vie Moderne* Monet exhibited eighteen works. The following list gives the numbers and titles (French) as they appeared in the catalogue of 1880. (Dates and identifications are those given in the Taschen edition of Wildenstein's catalogue raisonné.[115])

1. *Les Glaçons. Hiver de 1879-80. (The Ice Floes. Winter of 1879-80.)*
   1880. W. 568. Shelburne Museum of Art, Shelburne, Vermont (fig. 1)
2. *Corbeille de fruits. (Basket of Fruit.)*
   1880, begun in fall 1879. W. 546? Art Institute of Chicago (fig. 3)
3. *Pruniers en fleur. (Plum Trees in Flower.)*
   1879. W. 520? Szépmüvészeti Museum, Budapest, Hungary
4. *Route de la Roche-Guyon. (The Road to la Roche-Guyon.)*
   1880. W. 582. National Museum of Western Art, Tokyo
5. *La Prairie. (The Meadow.)*
   1879. W. 535? Joslyn Museum of Art, Omaha, Nebraska (fig. 4)
   Or 1879, but painted in 1880. W. 595? private collection, Germany
6. *Les Drapeaux. Rue Montorgueil, 30 juin 1878. (The Flags. Rue Montorgueil, June 30, 1878.)*
   1878. W. 469. Musée d'Orsay, Paris

7. *Le Givre. Effet de Soleil. (Frost, Sun Effect.)*
   1880. W. 555. Musée d'Orsay, Paris (Stuckey essay, fig. 10)
8. *Pommiers en fleur au bord de l'eau. (Apple Trees in Flower by the Edge of the Water.)*
   1880. W. 585. Private collection, France
9. *Le Verger. (The Orchard.)*
10. *Vue de Vétheuil. (View of Vétheuil.)*
11. *Après la débâcle. Hiver de 1879-80. (After the Débâcle. Winter of 1879-80.)*
12. *Gibier. (Game.)*
   1879. W. 551? Sale John T. Dorrance, New York, Sotheby's, October 18-19, 1989, no. 29
13. *Vétheuil, fin du jour. (Vétheuil, End of the Day.)*
   1880. W. 590. Private collection
14. *Le Givre. Temps gris. (Frost. Gray Weather.)*
   1879-1880. W. 553. Sale The Property of Michael Kroyer, Esq., London, Sotheby Parke Bernet, April 7, 1976, no. 19
15. *Marine. (Seascape.)*
   1867. W. 94. Musée d'Art et d'Histoire, Geneva
16. *La salle à manger. (The Dining Room.)*
   1868-69. W. 129? Bührle Foundation, Zurich
   Or 1868-69. W. 130? National Gallery of Art, Washington, D.C.
17. *Bateaux à Argenteuil. (Boats at Argenteuil.)*
18. *Gare Saint-Lazare. (Saint Lazare Train Station.)*

Ranging in date from 1867 to 1880, these constituted a sort of mini-retrospective, but the bulk of them were relatively recent landscapes done at Vétheuil. In addition to the painting that the Salon had rejected, *Les Glaçons* (no. 1 in the catalogue), there was another *Débâcle* scene (no. 11), as well as other Vétheuil landscapes done at different seasons and times of day (nos. 3, 4, 5, 8, 10, and 13), including two closely related variants of the same scene of frost (nos. 7 and 14), which brought to the fore the serial aspect of Monet's working method. Still lifes, which had been bringing higher prices to Monet than landscapes (see Stuckey essay, pp. 42 and 56), were also represented (nos. 2 and 12).

In organizing the exhibition, Duret and Hoschedé gathered some works from collectors, intentionally or not employing a strategy used by dealers to add prestige to the works in an exhibition.[116] Of the works in the show that have been identified, the

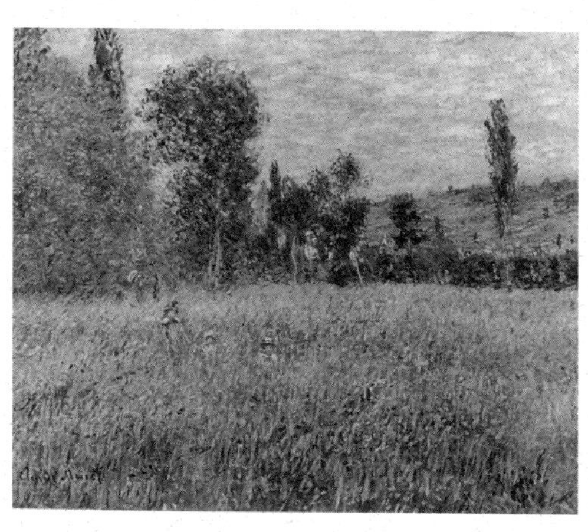

Fig. 4
Claude Monet
La Prairie
(The Meadow)
Ca. 1879
Oil on canvas
W. 535
Joslyn Art Museum, Omaha, Nebraska; Gift of William Averell Harriman

following were definitely borrowed from collectors: no. 6, *Les Drapeaux. Rue Montorgueil, 30 juin 1878*, lent by de Bellio; no. 7, *Le Givre, effet de Soleil*, lent by Caillebotte; no. 11, *Après la débâcle*, and no. 12, *Gibier*, both lent by Theulier; no. 15, *Marine*, lent by Duret; and no. 16, *Salle à manger*, lent by Depeaux or Deudon, depending on which painting this was.[117] Of course, the organizers may have been limited to what could easily be borrowed in Paris at relatively short notice. It may have been a matter of chance or a wise move to include one of two paintings of flags displayed in Paris on June 30, 1878 (no. 6), previously shown in the Impressionist group show of 1879. These had been praised in the press both by Burty and Silvestre,[118] critics who had otherwise been harsh.

Despite Duret's claim that Monet worked only outdoors and not in the studio, the show included works of various degrees of finish, as noted by Spate. Not only were there more completely worked up paintings, but also more sketchily rendered ones, as evocatively described by Burty in his review in *La République Française*, of the works that attracted him most in the show: "fragments of incontestable power" (*morceaux d'incontestable puissance*).[119]

Spate also suggests that the sketchy, though carefully constructed *Soleil couchant sur la Seine, effet d'hiver*, now in the Musée du Petit Palais (fig. 2), was included in the exhibition.[120] She apparently is referring to no. 11, *Après la débâcle. Hiver de 1879-80*. But this must be one of two paintings that Theulier lent to the show,[121] and he is not thought to have owned the one at the Petit Palais.

Moreover, Spate asserts that several of the works formed a subgroup dealing with the theme of the family and were included in the show to suggest that Monet was a family man and thereby refute rumors about Monet's living arrangement. This idea is not fully persuasive. While the *Salle à manger* (no. 16) clearly shows a family group, it is highly speculative to suggest that the still life of dead game birds (no. 12) is symbolic of Monet's family before Camille died. And Spate's reference to "one of the first paintings of his reconstituted family in 1880" (apparently no. 5) is problematic, for we are not sure which one of perhaps two paintings this was (W. 535? [fig. 4] or W. 595?).[122]

The new strategies represented in the mounting and publicizing of the *Vie Moderne* show bore fruit almost immediately. During the run of the show, several collectors showed interest in acquiring *Les Glaçons*.[123] Among these was Madame Charpentier, whose husband had admired the work while it hung in the gallery. In her letter of June 22, 1880 to Monet, she told him about her husband's enthusiasm for the painting, which she would like to acquire. However, she wrote that she could not afford the price of the painting, which she would have to buy out of her household savings (2000 francs was the asking price at the gallery); instead, she proposed to pay 1500 francs in installments.[124] Alice Hoschedé was quick with a negative reaction; in a letter to Hoschedé of about June 23, 1880, she complained about the installment plan and the amount, which would not bring any profit. She also said that before responding to Madame Charpentier, Monet would offer the painting to Ratisbonne and Ephrussi, who also showed interest in buying the painting.[125] But by the time he answered Madame Charpentier on June 27, Monet had come up with a way to earn a profit. He wrote that he had promised to offer the painting to another buyer, but since that person was absent, she could have the painting; however, to allow him a profit, he would like

Fig. 5
Claude Monet
Account book
Pages for April–June 1880, folios 28v-29
Musée Marmottan, Paris.

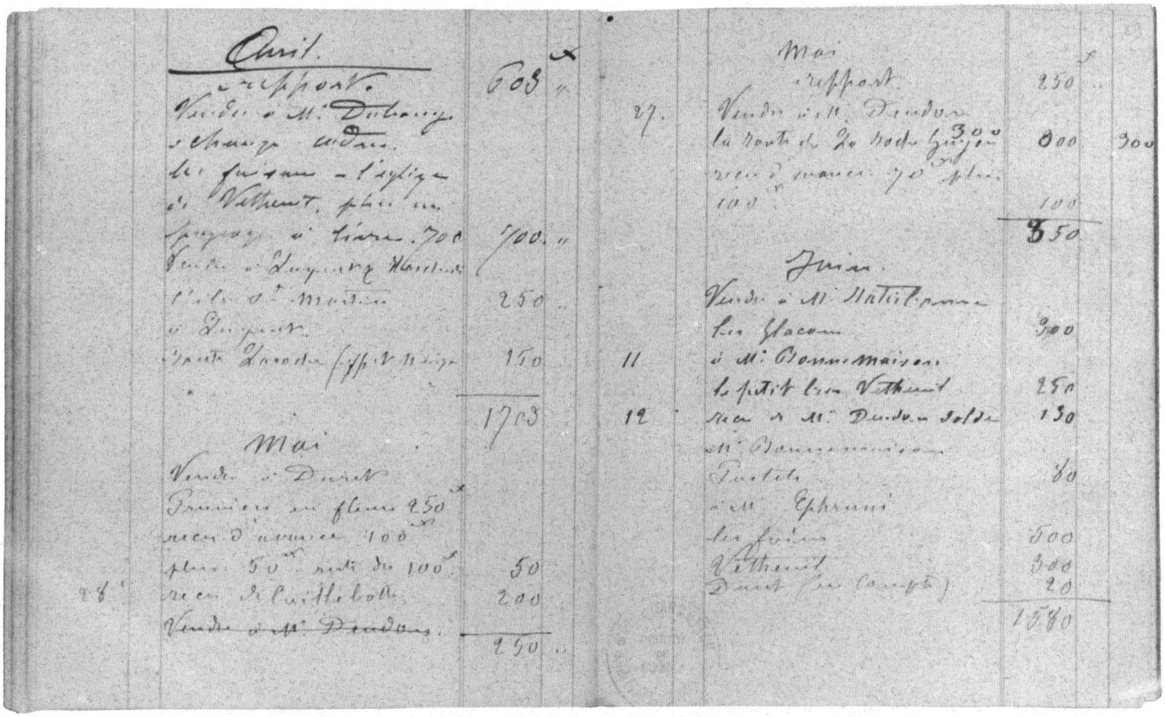

her to forgo the gallery's fifteen percent commission. He added that he was delighted to know that his painting would be at her house (he would have been aware of the prominent visitors—and potential patrons—who might see it there).[126]

Other collectors, such as the aforementioned Ratisbonne and Ephrussi, bought paintings. Landscapes went for far more than the 150 francs that Petit and de Bellio had paid several months earlier. For June 1880 Monet recorded the sale of a painting entitled *Les Glaçons* (it is unclear which one) to Ratisbonne for 300 francs. (See fig. 5.) Later in December that patron bought a painting of flowers for 500 francs.[127]

The case of Charles Ephrussi (critic at the *Gazette des Beaux-Arts*, of which he later became co-owner)[128] is interesting because just a few years earlier, he had considered the paintings of Monet and his colleagues too summary.[129] The *Vie Moderne* exhibition may have contributed to reversing Ephrussi's opinion, since that collector's first purchase from Monet took place during the run of the show.[130] On June 12 Monet recorded in his account book that he had sold two paintings to Ephrussi: *Les Foins (Hay)*, for 500 francs (possibly no. 5 of the *Vie Moderne* exhibition, *La Prairie*)[131] and *Vétheuil* for 300 francs. (See fig. 5.) In July the sale of *Paysage île St-Martin (Landscape, Île Saint-Martin)* for 400 francs is recorded; this must be the painting Monet aimed to be working on in letters to Ephrussi.[132] In December Monet recorded an exchange of one painting for another with Ephrussi. This may have been *Pommiers (Apple Trees)*, which was later seen by Ephrussi's secretary, the poet Jules Laforgue, at Ephrussi's house in 1881.[133] Alternatively, the exchange in December may have been for *Les Glaçons* (*The Ice Floes*, W. 567, pl. 5) now at the Musée d'Orsay, the sketch for the large painting sold to the Charpentiers;[134] both were shown in Monet's exhibition at Georges Petit's in 1889. Much later, Ephrussi's secretary Marcel Proust, who came to work for him in 1896, alluded to the Orsay *Glaçons* in several works, including *Jean Santeuil, Contre Sainte-Beuve*, as well as *Le Côté de Guermantes* and its preliminary texts.[135]

In a clear marketing ploy, an anonymous article published in *La Vie Moderne* asserted that all the works in the show had been sold,[136] which was patently untrue since a good portion of the works had been lent. Cézanne, in a letter to Zola of June 19, 1880 wrote: "Monet now has a splendid showing at Charpentier's gallery, *La Vie Moderne*. . . . ," and two weeks later, in early July: "Monet, according to what I've heard, has sold some of the canvases that were shown at Monsieur Charpentier's. . . ."[137] Monet, in a letter of July 5, complained to Duret that he could have sold more if people had not already owned the works. He said he had received several letters from new collectors interested in Duret's seascape, the Gare Saint-Lazare, and several other paintings. He said he had sold *Les Glaçons* to Madame Charpentier, who was offering it to her husband; he also sold a new painting to Ephrussi but unfortunately everyone was disappearing.[138] Nevertheless, having works in the show that others owned seems to have had the effect of encouraging the sales of works not in the show (as we have seen for the Ratisbonne and Ephrussi purchases noted above), and Monet held court in the flat in the rue Vintimille where he kept works to show.[139] Alice's letter to Ernest of about June 23 asking him to try to get Monet's show extended speaks of the painter's need for more time in order to finish some more paintings. This flurry of painting activity must have been a reaction to positive interest of people at the *Vie Moderne* show.

Other collectors who bought works around the time of the show were Bonnemaison (a landscape for 250 francs and pastels for 80 francs), Coqueret (a landscape for 200 francs), and Monsieur and Madame Serveau (a landscape for 300 francs and a portrait for 150 francs). In October, Delius, a new patron,[140] bought two still lifes of fruit for 1400 francs. A work listed as no. 2 in the exhibition, *Corbeille de fruits*, may have been one of three that Cahuzac bought for 1000 francs from the artist in November; possibly this was *Nature morte: pommes et raisin* (*Still Life: Apples and Grapes*), now at the Art Institute of Chicago (W. 546, fig. 3).[141]

Critical Reaction

While the reviews that the *Vie Moderne* show received were not substantial, some noted daring qualities of Monet's art, such as sketchiness and decorativeness, indicating that these long-derided traits were becoming more acceptable. Burty, writing in *La République Française* in 1880, drew attention to certain works, acknowledging an attraction to paintings that were not fully rendered.[142]

An anonymous reviewer, probably Alfred de Lostalot,[143] in *La Chronique des Arts et de la Curiosité* of June 1880, gave a general, but favorable, assessment of the show: "Among the eighteen paintings exhibited, there are some remarkable ones. Without going into an appreciation of the aesthetics of the painter, we can acknowledge his rare talent as a landscapist and the skillfulness with which he uses the most radical practices of Impressionism."[144] Lostalot's juxtaposition of skill and radicality suggests a new appreciation of Monet's art, an evolution from his lukewarm reaction to the painter's work in 1876. Lostalot's positive attitude (if indeed he was the writer) would blossom into significant support for Monet in 1883 and beyond.[145]

Among the highlights of the exhibition cited by the anonymous article in *La Vie Moderne* on June 19, 1880 were: "*The Thaw in the Setting Sun*, a very important canvas, whose effect could not be more decorative; different views of Vétheuil at various times; the *Boats of Argenteuil,* whose brilliancy and reflections recall Venetian coloration" (le Dégel au soleil couchant, *tableau très important et d'un effet on ne peut plus décoratif; diverses vues de Vétheuil à des heures variées;* les Bateaux d'Argenteuil, *dont l'éclat et les reflects rappellent les colorations vénitiennes*). Levine has noted that this passage presents succinctly the formal concerns that would be addressed in the criticism of Monet's painting over the next thirty years: "its largeness of scale, decorative effect, series format, and color independent of form."[146] In particular, the reviewer's remark concerning the decorative qualities of *Les Glaçons*[147] is intriguing because he uses this term positively. This term had been derogatory in Impressionist criticism since Silvestre first used it in 1874 to categorize an overall patternlike use of color rather than reliance on line as the basis for composition.[148] Here the use of the term heralds the positive connotations that it was to attain later in the 1880s and 1890s.[149]

Later *Les Glaçons* was singled out in reviews that reflect currents of naturalism. Regarding the seventh Impressionist group exhibition in 1882, Silvestre (who had, on the occasion of the fourth Impressionist group exhibition in 1879, noted a lack of new direction in Monet's Vétheuil paintings) now wrote in the journal *La Vie Moderne*:[150] "There is more real harmony in a landscape of M. Claude Monet than in all the entries for the Rome prize in ten years. . . ." For Silvestre, Monet's naturalism showed his poetic powers; the reviewer thus adumbrated the affinities that Symbolist poets would find in Monet:[151] "For me Monet is not only the most exquisite of the Impressionists, but also one of the true contemporary poets of the things of nature; he not only paints it, he sings it; a lyre seems to be hidden in his palette." Silvestre drew attention to several paintings, including the *Glaçons*: "I've kept for the end *Les Glaçons*, a canvas of a marvelous accuracy of impression and of an immense decorative effect." Here Silvestre lauded both the naturalism and the decorativeness of Monet's painting, though, as Levine has pointed out, for Silvestre the latter quality had not entirely lost its negative connotations.[152] Noting the great success that *Les Glaçons* had earned in the *Vie Moderne* show, Armand Sallanches, in *Le Journal des Arts*, commented on the realistic aspects of the painting, while criticizing its color: "In the first rank let us mention *Les Glaçons*, a restrained and robust painting that you admire the more you look at it. The trees are really planted, and the ice is really swept along by the water that really reflects the landscape. One criticism—Monet sees too much red-currant color."[153]

Joris-Karl Huysmans, who in 1880 had complained that Monet produced "uncertain approximations" (*incertaines abréviations*),[154] cited *Les Glaçons*, in his 1882 review of the Impressionist group show, as evidence for Monet's having reached a turning point with respect to more complete and less sketchy painting and better use of color. "Fortunately Monet's had a turning point; it seems he's decided no longer to daub piles of paintings. He's recovered and has given us this time very beautiful and very complete landscapes."[155] Huysmans also praised Monet's capacity to endow his painting with emotion[156] as well as render qualities of light convincingly: "His ice-floes beneath a reddish-brown sky are of an intense melancholy. . . . Certainly, the painter who brushed these paintings is a great landscapist whose eye, now healed, seizes with a surprising faithfulness all phenomena of light. . . ."

Conclusion

Monet's new mode of exhibition did not immediately come to dominate his thinking. Even at the moment when Monet was planning his *Vie Moderne* exhibition, he still held on to the idea of eventual Salon success, for in May 1880 he and Renoir sent a protest to Minister of Fine Arts Jules Ferry, demanding a showing at the next Salon "in suitable circumstances."[157] This request suggests Monet's continued ambivalence about which exhibition route he should follow.

It was not until the dealer Durand-Ruel—when he was financially able in 1881 and had begun buying up works by Impressionist painters—began to purchase works from Monet in bulk, including *La Débâcle (The Breakup of the Ice)*, now at the University of Michigan Museum of Art (W. 565, pl. 3), and offered him a contract with monthly stipends, that Monet decided not to enter the Salon. The Salon, as a government-sponsored event, ended that year, as well. Monet spent a significant portion of the rest of his career playing one dealer against another. The format of the one-man retrospective at Durand-Ruel's and at Petit's fit well with Monet's series productions of the 1890s and beyond. The *Vie Moderne* exhibition was a harbinger of this later practice.

Les Glaçons, that exhibition's centerpiece, exercised a tenacious hold on the way Monet wanted himself represented over the next decade. The painting was subsequently borrowed for two important exhibitions. Monet expressed enthusiasm about the work when he asked Durand-Ruel to ask Madame Charpentier to lend it to the 1882 Impressionist group show.[158] The Salon's rejection was again held up as a badge of honor in his 1889 retrospective at Petit's, where the painting was noted in the catalogue as being "the work rejected by the Salon" (*le refusé du Salon*), almost a decade after its refusal by the jury.

Notes

I am indebted to Charles Stuckey and Carole McNamara for numerous invaluable discussions pertaining to Monet in general and to issues raised in this article. I am grateful to James Manheim for his thoughtful and insightful reading of my text in its various phases. I would also like to express my appreciation to Rachel Vez Fridrich for the many hours that she spent assisting in the research for the Monet project and for her diligence in ordering photographs and preparing the captions for the illustrations in this catalogue.

1 Now at the Dallas Museum of Art.

2 Unless otherwise indicated, identifications of paintings are those in Daniel Wildenstein, *Claude Monet: Biographie et catalogue raisonné* (Lausanne, 1974), vol. 1.

3 Now at the Shelburne Museum, Shelburne, Vermont.

4 Émile Zola, "Le Naturalisme au Salon," *Le Voltaire* (June 18-22, 1880), *Écrits sur l'art*, ed. Jean-Pierre Leduc-Adine ([Paris], 1991), 418.

5 Lionello Venturi, *Les Archives de l'Impressionnisme: Lettres de Renoir, Monet, Pissarro, Sisley et autres. Mémoires de Paul Durand-Ruel. Documents*, 2 vols. (Paris and New York, 1939), 1:229-230, letter 20.

6 Émile Taboureux, "Claude Monet," *La Vie Moderne* (June 12, 1880): 380, 382 (translated in Charles F. Stuckey, ed., *Monet: A Retrospective*, New York, 1985, 89-93).

7 Théodore Duret, *Le Peintre Claude Monet: Notice sur son oeuvre, par Théodore Duret, suivie du catalogue de ses tableaux exposés dans la galerie du journal illustré, La Vie Moderne, 7, boulevard des Italiens, 7, le 7 juin 1880 et jours suivants* (Paris, 1880). Duret's essay was later published in his *Critique d'avant-garde* (Paris, 1885), 93-105 (translated in Stuckey 1985, 70-72).

8 This was a claim made earlier on behalf of the Impressionists in general by their supporters. Duret, "Les Peintres Impressionnistes" ([Paris], 1878), in *idem* 1885, 57-89, discusses their originality in painting out-of-doors (a portion is translated in Stuckey 1985, 65-67). Edmond Renoir, "Les Impressionnistes," *La Presse* (April 11, 1879): 2, noted that the Impressionists rejected the atelier; Zola, "Nouvelles artistiques et littéraires," *Le Messager de l'Europe* (July 1879), in Leduc-Adine, 399-400, valued the Impressionists for their work outside in natural light.

9 Wildenstein 1974, 1:109; John House, *Nature into Art* (New Haven and London, 1986), 147, 153; Joel Isaacson, "The Painters Called Impressionists," in San Francisco, Fine Arts Museums of San Francisco, and Washington, DC, National Gallery of Art, *The New Painting, Impressionism 1874-1886*, Charles S. Moffett *et al.*, exh. cat., 2nd ed., San Francisco, 1986, 385 and 392, n. 69; Steven Z. Levine, *Monet, Narcissus, and Self-Reflection: The Modernist Myth of the Self* (Chicago and London, 1994), 23.

10 Wildenstein 1974, 1:288.

11 *Ibid.* 1:294, 296.

12 *Ibid.* 1: 304.

13 House 1986, 140; Virginia Spate, *Claude Monet: Life and Work* (New York, 1992), 141-143; and Levine 1994, 23 and *passim*. This idea was briefly set forth in Wildenstein 1974, 1:111-112.

14 Earlier one-man shows include Manet's and Courbet's in 1867, Whistler's in 1874, and Daumier's in 1878. John Rewald, *The History of Impressionism*, 4th rev. ed., The Museum of Modern Art (New York, 1973), 430, notes the rarity of one-artist exhibitions at this time. On the emergence of solo exhibitions at Paris dealers in the early 1880s, see Martha Ward, "Impressionist Installations and Private Exhibitions," *The Art Bulletin* 73, no. 4 (December 1991): 613, 615-618. On the novelty of Durand-Ruel's one-man shows in the 1890s and on the presentation of Monet's series paintings there during that decade, see House, "Time's Cycles," *Art in America* 80 (October 1992): 126-135, 161.

15 See Levine, *Monet and His Critics*, Ph.D. diss., Harvard University, 1974 (New York and London, 1976), 33-37.

16 Letter of June 23, 1880 from Alice Hoschedé to her husband Ernest. See Wildenstein 1974, 1:446, *pièce justificative* 46.

17 Pissarro, in a letter of 1878 to Caillebotte, recounted this observation by Monet; see *Correspondance de Camille Pissarro*, ed. Janine Bailly-Herzberg (Paris, 1980) 1:109-110, letter 53.

18 For Caillebotte's letter to Monet, from the end of March 1879, see Marie Berhaut, *Caillebotte, sa vie et son oeuvre: Catalogue raisonné des peintures et pastels* (Paris, 1978), 244-245, letter 15.

19 Levine 1976 extensively analyzes the issue of facture with respect to Monet; for Levine's comments on Zola and Wolff, see pp. 34-35, 37. On critics' discussions of sketches and studies in academic and Impressionist painting, see Richard Shiff, *Cézanne and the End of Impressionism: A Study of the Theory, Technique, and Critical Evaluation of Modern Art* (Chicago and London, 1984), chap. 7. For a discussion of terms as they apply to Monet see House 1986, chap. 9.

20 Albert Wolff, "Les Indépendants," *Le Figaro* (April 11, 1879): 1.

21 Zola 1879, in Leduc-Adine, 399-400.

22 Armand Silvestre, "Le Monde des arts: Les Indépendants.—Les Aquarellistes," *La Vie Moderne* (April 24, 1879): 38.

23 *Idem*, Preface, *Galerie Durand-Ruel: Recueil d'estampes gravées à l'eau-forte* (Paris, 1873), 22, as cited in Levine 1976, 14 and 420, n. 21. Silvestre's preface was first published serially in *La Renaissance littéraire et artistique* (August 17-September 28, 1872), as noted in Chicago, The Art Institute of Chicago, *Claude Monet 1840-1926*, exh. cat. by Charles F. Stuckey, July 22-November 26, 1995 (Chicago, 1995), 197.

24 Wolff, 1. Levine 1976, 37-38, makes this point, noting that Monet's reflection of some of the critic's words in his interview with Taboureux suggests that he must have known Wolff's article (see below n. 99); Levine says that Monet probably would have known Wolff's article through newspaper clippings that Caillebotte would have given him.

25 London, Hayward Gallery, and Boston, Museum of Fine Arts, *Impressions of France: Monet, Renoir, Pissarro, and their Rivals*, exh. cat. by House *et al.* (London, 1995), 50, 51, and 136, no. 28.

26 Anne Distel, *Les collectionneurs des impressionnistes: amateurs et marchands* (Düdingen/Guin, 1989), 60. See, e.g., Duret's letter of February 15, 1874 on this subject to Pissarro; Ludovic Rodo[lphe] Pissarro and Lionello Venturi, *Camille Pissarro: Son art—son oeuvre* (Paris, 1939), 1:33-34. For Duret as a collector see Distel, 57-71; Yvon Bizardel, "Théodore Duret. An Early Friend of the Impressionists," *Apollo* (August 1974): 146-155.

27 Wildenstein 1974, 1:438, letter 173.

28 Letter to Georges de Bellio (Wildenstein 1974, 1:438, letter 170) and unpublished letter to Duret at The Pierpont Morgan Library, New York (see below, n. 113), both written on January 8, 1880. I thank Charles Stuckey for kindly bringing the Duret letter to my attention; I am grateful to Robert E. Parks of the Morgan Library for making available to me copies of this letter and others relating to Monet in the Adolphe Tabarant papers. On the issue of selling for lower prices, Monet's letter to de Bellio indicates that he had just sold to that collector "one of the best and most important of my canvases," a "Vue de Vétheuil" *(View of Vétheuil)* [possibly the painting now at the Art Gallery of Ontario, Toronto (W. 534, pl. 9)] for 150 francs, the same price that Petit had paid for each of the landscapes that he had bought, but far less than de Bellio's landscape was worth.

29 Rewald 1973, 434, suggests that Petit made Salon entry a condition for further purchases; concrete evidence is available only in Monet's letter to Duret of March 8, 1880 (see above n. 27).

30 See Wildenstein 1974, 1:106 and 446, *pièces justificatives* 38 and 41.

31 "La Journée parisienne, Impression d'un Impressionniste," *Le Gaulois* (January 24, 1880), as cited and discussed in Wildenstein 1974, 1:107-108 and n. 799-803; translated in Stuckey 1985, 69-70.

32 Wildenstein 1974, 1:108.

33 We know of Monet's letter from de Bellio's response; see Wildenstein 1974, 1:108 and n. 806.

34 Letter of February 2, 1880 to Pissarro (Wildenstein 1974, 1:108 and 438, letter 172).

35 See n. 27 above.

36 Venturi, 1:46. Citing Venturi, Rewald 1973, 434, and Wildenstein 1974, 1: 111 and n. 839, assume that Degas was referring only to the half-success at the Salon, while Spate, 141, thinks that Degas' remark covers both the Salon submission as well as the *Vie Moderne* show and publications.

37 Isaacson, "*La Débâcle* by Claude Monet," *Bulletin, Museums of Art and Archaeology, The University of Michigan* 1 (1978): 7, notes that both paintings fit Monet's phrase; cf. *idem* in San Francisco and Washington 1986, 385. Los Angeles, Los Angeles County Museum of Art, Chicago, The Art Institute of Chicago, and Paris, Réunion des Musées Nationaux, *A Day in the Country: Impressionism and the French Landscape*, exh. cat. by Richard Brettell *et al.* (Los Angeles, 1984), 168, no. 55, argues that this phrase described *Les Glaçons*. House 1986, 153, 166, 208, thinks the reference was to *Lavacourt*; see also House *et al.*, in London and Boston 1995, 136, no. 36, for the same opinion.

38 See Isaacson 1978, 7; *idem* in San Francisco and Washington 1986, 385; Brettell *et al.* in Los Angeles, Chicago, and Paris 1984, 168, no. 55; Spate, 140; House *et al.* in London and Boston 1995, 136, no. 36.

39 Noted by House *et al.* in London and Boston 1995, 136, no. 36.

40 Noted by Brettell *et al.* in Los Angeles, Chicago, and Paris 1984, 168, no. 55.

41 Noted by Isaacson 1978, 7; see also *idem* in San Francisco and Washington 1986, 385.

42 For Cézanne's letter of May 10, 1880 to Zola, see *Paul Cézanne: Letters*, ed. John Rewald, trans. by Seymour Hacker, rev. and augm. ed. (New York, 1984), 189-190. For Zola's reply of May 13, 1880 to Cézanne, see Rewald 1984., 190-191.

43 Zola 1880, in Leduc-Adine, 409-438.

44 *Ibid.*, 418.

45 *Ibid.*, 425-426.

46 Levine 1976, 40.

47 Wildenstein 1974, 1:364, notes that these were W. 475 and W. 538-540.

48 Philippe de Chennevières, "Salon de 1880," *Gazette des Beaux-Arts* 22 (July 1880): 44.

49 Levine 1976, 41.

50 Philippe Burty, "Le Salon de 1880: Lettres des jurés—les paysages," *L'Art* 21 (1880): 231.

51 *Idem*, "Le Salon de 1880," *La République Française* (June 19, 1880), as cited in Levine 1976, 42; a portion is translated in Stuckey 1985, 93.

52 Edmond Renoir, "Le peintre Renoir—Lettre à Émile Bergerat," *La Vie Moderne* (June 19, 1879); reprinted in Venturi, 2:334-338.

53 Adolphe Tabarant, *Manet et ses oeuvres*, ([Paris], 1947), 367, gives the checklist from the catalogue but mentions no essay. The review was by Gustave Goetschy, "Édouard Manet," *La Vie Moderne* (April 17, 1880), 247-250; George Heard Hamilton, *Manet and His Critics* (New Haven and London, 1954), 227-228, describes the review and gives an excerpt from it; Anne Coffin Hanson, *Manet and the Modern Tradition* (New Haven and London), 132-133, also discusses the review.

54 Rewald, "Auguste Renoir and His Brother," *Gazette des Beaux-Arts* 27 (March 1945): 182; Distel, 142. For further information on Madame Charpentier's salon, see Michel Robida, *Le Salon Charpentier et les impressionnistes*, Paris, 1958; Georges Rivière, *Renoir et ses amis*, Paris, 1921, esp. chap. X, "Les soirées chez Mme Charpentier."

55 Rewald 1945, 183.

56 Hanson, 130, n. 352.

57 Distel, 145-146.

58 Hanson, 40, 130-131.

59 Silvestre, *La Vie Moderne* (April 10, 1879): 6, as cited and translated in Hanson, 130.

60 Rewald 1945, 183.

61 *Ibid.*

62 *Ibid.*

63 See note 14 above.

64 As cited and translated by Rewald 1945, 183.

65 Rivière 1921, 178, 180; *idem*, "Claude Monet aux expositions des Impressionnistes," *L'Art vivant* 3, no. 49 (January 1, 1927): 18 (portions translated in Stuckey 1985, 63-64).

66 Rewald 1945, 184.

67 *Ibid.*

68 See Tabarant, 375-377; Hamilton, 226-227.

69 Wildenstein 1974, 1:439, letter 179, written on May 19, 1880.

70 Wildenstein, *Monet: Catalogue raisonné, Werkverzeichnis*, trans. Josephine Bacon (Cologne, 1996), 2: 114 (W. 264), 146 (W. 354), 174 (W. 427).

71 Wildenstein 1974, 1:430, letters 91 and 92; 431, letter 96; see also 445, *pièce justificative* 29; 447, *pièce justificative* 68.

72 Venturi 2:260, no. 106 of exh. Michel Rostand, *Quelques amateurs de l'époque impressionniste*, unpublished thesis, École du Louvre, 1955, 241 and n. 2, thought that this was Charpentier's first purchase. I am grateful to Michel Rostand for kindly granting me permission to consult his thesis at the Archives du Musée du Louvre. However, this painting is not included among those identified as belonging to Charpentier in Wildenstein's index listing; see Wildenstein 1974, 1:454 (these are: W. 264, W. 354, W. 427, and W. 568).

73 Rostand, 240; Wildenstein 1974, 1: 431, letter 102; 435, letter 142.

74 Wildenstein 1974, 1:435, letter 145.

75 As we infer from Monet's letter of January 24, 1879 to Charpentier; *ibid.*, 1:436, letter 152.

76 Letter of October 13, 1879; *ibid.*, 1:438, letter 166.

77 Rewald 1945, 182, says that Renoir had met the Charpentiers before the Franco-Prussian war. Joel Isaacson, *Observation and Reflection: Claude Monet* (Oxford and New York, 1978), 23, holds that Renoir secured the exhibition for Monet. Marianne Alphant, *Claude Monet, une vie dans le paysage* (Paris, 1993), 318, assumes that it was Renoir who got the show for Monet since he had introduced Monet to the Charpentiers.

78 Rewald 1973, 431.

79 Wildenstein 1974, 1:110 and n. 823, notes Guillemet's letter to Manet of April 7, 1880. On this letter see Tabarant, 377-378. The date of this letter indicates how early the results could have been made known to colleagues.

80 For example, at the end of 1877, with Monet in desperate straits, Manet wrote to Duret to see if they both could respond to Monet's

request for a bulk purchase of his paintings, each of them contributing 500 francs. While Manet made the contribution, Duret was unable to; Manet probably never took the paintings. See Rewald 1973, 412.

81 See Tabarant, 375.

82 On Duret, see n. 26 above; on Hoschedé, see Hélène Adhémar, "Ernest Hoschedé," in *Aspects of Monet: A Symposium on the Artist's Life and Times*, ed. John Rewald and Frances Weitzenhoffer (New York, 1984), 53-71.

83 Charles Léger, *Claude Monet* (Paris, 1930), 9.

84 Duret, *Histoire d'Édouard Manet et de son oeuvre* (Paris, 1902), 129, says that Charpentier organized the show because he thought that it would be useful to Monet and Impressionist art. (It seems more likely that Charpentier would have been persuaded on these points rather than that he himself would have been the instigator.)

85 Only a summary of this letter is given in Wildenstein 1974, 1:439, letter, 176. We know that the letter was written in April because it refers to the visit that reporter Émile Taboureux had just made to interview Monet in connection with the show. In the resulting article Taboureux, 380, refers to the "April sun" (*soleil aprilien*). See Wildenstein 1974, 1:111.

86 Wildenstein 1974, 1:439, letter 179, written on May 19, 1880.

87 See letter to de Bellio of March 10, 1879, *ibid.*, 1:436, letter 155; letter of Alice Hoschedé of just before March 15, 1880 to her husband Ernest, *ibid.*, 1:446, *pièce justificative* 44. See Levine 1994, *passim*, on this aspect of Monet's personality.

88 Monet mentioned Hoschedé in a letter of May 22,1880 to Duret (Wildenstein 1974, 1:439, letter 180).

89 Letter of May 24, 1880; *ibid.*, 1:439, letter 181.

90 Letter to Duret, May 27, 1880; *ibid.*, letter 182.

91 Letter to Duret, May 29, 1880; *ibid.*, letter 183.

92 Letter to Duret, June 4, 1880; *ibid.*, letter 184.

93 *Ibid.*, 1:440, letter 191.

94 Duret 1902, 130, later said that Charpentier himself asked him to write the essay and had the catalogue printed up. Duret also related that the public came only to laugh at and mock the exhibition, and no one would buy the catalogue at 50 centimes; when the price was lowered to 10 centimes, there were a few buyers. Toward the end of the show, Charpentier decided that they would give the catalogue away, but most people refused. However, in 1899 Duret ran across a copy of the catalogue being sold in a bookshop as a rarity, at one franc.

95 See Nicholas Green, "Economic Transformation of the Artistic Field in France during the Second Half of the Nineteenth Century," *Art History* 10, no. 1 (March 1987): 65, 69-72, esp. p. 69, on the cachet of art historians' introductions that used the biography of an artist to tout his individual creativity and uniqueness.

96 Cf. Levine 1994, 23.

97 Taboureux, 380. The translation is that of Levine 1994, 23.

98 Cf. Isaacson in San Francisco and Washington 1986, 385 and 392, n. 68, for a consideration of the relationship of Monet's words to Impressionist theory and practice.

99 Taboureux, 380. Monet's phrases "la petite église" and "premier barbouilleur venu" reflect some of Wolff's words in his article (see n. 20 and 24 above) criticizing the Impressionist show of 1879; Levine 1976, 37-38, suggests that Wolff's article was, therefore, likely on Monet's mind when he made the decision to enter the Salon.

100 Alphant, 318.

101 Rewald 1973, 447.

102 Taboureux, 382.

103 Duret 1880; *idem* 1885, 93-105. See above, n. 7.

104 Noted by Levine 1976, 43.

105 Duret 1880, 6-7.

106 "... une peinture à l'huile tout entière commencée et terminée devant la scène naturelle, directement interprétée et rendue." *Ibid.*, 7.

107 "... il travaille en toute saison directement sous la voûte du ciel. Sur son chevalet il pose une toile blanche, et il commence brusquement à la couvrir de plaques de couleur qui correspondent aux taches colorées que lui donne la scène naturelle entrevue. Souvent, pendant la première séance, il n'a pu obtenir qu'une ébauche. Le lendemain, revenu sur les lieux, il ajoute à la première esquisse, et les détails s'accentuent, les contours se précisent. Il procède ainsi plus ou moins jusqu'à ce que le tableau le satisfasse." *Ibid.*, 10.

108 *Ibid.*, 9-10. Levine 1976, 44-45, suggests that Duret implies that Monet has established a new kind of *tableau.*

109 Wildenstein 1974, 1:364.

110 *Ibid.*, 1:360.

111 Noted by Spate, 142. For the letter, see above n. 27.

112 Wildenstein 1974, 1:106.

113 "J'ai naturellement essayé de faire une toile de cela, mais ça [the thaw] été (sic) si rapide que je n'ai pu faire qu'une esquisse"; from an unpublished letter to Duret of January 8, 1880 (The Pierpont Morgan Library, New York, MA 3950. See above, n. 28).

114 Cf. Spate, 142.

115 Wildenstein 1996, vol. 2.

116 On this practice among dealers, see Green, 64.

117 Durand-Ruel first owned both of these paintings; we do not know when they passed to their subsequent owners. Owing to the poor relationship that Monet and this dealer appear to have had between December 1873 and February 1881 (see Stuckey essay, pp. 46-48, 50, 60-61), it seems unlikely that Durand-Ruel would have lent to this show.

118 Burty, "L'Exposition des artistes indépendants," *La République Française* (April 16, 1879):3, as cited in Levine 1976, 36; reprinted in Ruth Berson, *The New Painting, Impressionism 1874-1886. Documentation. Volume I: Reviews*, Fine Arts Museums of San Francisco, San Francisco, 1996, 209-210. Silvestre 1879, 38.

119 See n. 51 above; Spate, 143, cites Burty's preference for the sketchier works.

120 *Ibid.*, 141-143; cf. Isaacson in San Francisco and Washington 1986, 385.

121 Wildenstein 1974, 1:439, letter 183.

122 See Spate, 143; see also p. 138.

123 Soon after the Salon results were out, Murer expressed interest in acquiring one of the Salon submissions, apparently in repayment for a 50-franc debt. In response to this letter from Murer, Monet replied, in a letter of April 9, 1880 that each painting would be 1500 francs, thus Murer would owe him 1450 francs (Wildenstein 1974, 1:439, letter 175). We infer from the letter that Madame Charpentier wrote on June 22 1880, during the *Vie Moderne* show, that the asking price of *Les Glaçons* had gone up for the show to 2000 francs (*ibid.*, 1:446, *pièce justificative* 45). In a letter a few months later to Murer, Monet offered him two other works (*ibid.*, 1:440, letter 189).

124 *Ibid.*, 1:446, *pièce justificative* 45.

125 See n. 16 above.

126 Wildenstein 1974, 1:440, letter 186.

127 This is possibly W. 627, as suggested by *ibid*, 1:113, n. 854.

128 On Ephrussi see Jean-Paul Bouillon *et al.*, *La Promenade du critique influent: Anthologie de*

la critique d'art en France, 1850-1900 (Paris, 1990), 223. On Ephrussi's collecting see Distel, 160-162; see also Philippe Kolb and Jean Adhémar, "Charles Ephrussi (1849-1905), ses secrétaires: Laforgue, A. Renan, Proust, 'sa' Gazette des Beaux-Arts," *Gazette des Beaux-Arts* 103 (January 1984): 29-41.

129 Charles Ephrussi, "*Les Peintres impressionnistes. . . ,* par Théodore Duret," *La Chronique des Arts et de la Curiosité* (May 18, 1878): 158.

130 Distel, 162, notes that Ephrussi's purchases began in 1880. Kolb and Adhémar, 39-40, n. 13, are incorrect that Ephrussi acquired *Les Glaçons*, W. 556, in January 1879, for that painting was purchased by Paindessous then; see Wildenstein 1974, 1:354 ("Pindessous" is corrected to "Paindessous" in the Taschen ed.). *Idem* 1974, 1:455 (index) lists the following works in Ephrussi's collection: W. 135?, W. 377?, W. 489?, W. 567, W. 592?, W. 595. (This list is different from the works that Kolb and Adhémar write that Wildenstein cites.)

131 Suggested in Wildenstein 1996, 2:230, W. 595, *Vétheuil vu de l'île Saint-Martin (Vétheuil Seen from Île Saint Martin)*, now in a private collection in Germany. See *idem* 1974, 1:439, letter 185.

132 Suggested in *idem* 1996, 2:229, W. 592, *Sentier dans les coquelicots, île Saint-Martin (Lane in the Poppy Field, Île Saint-Martin)*, now at the Metropolitan Museum of Art. See also *idem* 1974, 1:113 and n. 854; 1:440, letters 188 and 191. Wildenstein 1996, 2:229, also suggests that this purchase was W. 593, *Champ de coquelicots près de Vétheuil (Poppy Field Near Vétheuil)*, whose last known location was a private collection in Switzerland in 1956.

133 W. 489. *Idem* 1974, 1:446, *pièce justificative* 49.

134 According to *idem* 1996, 2:221. But this edition of Wildenstein apparently errs in suggesting the month of May as well for the exchange, as Monet's account book has no mention of a transaction with Ephrussi at that time.

135 As established by J. Theodore Johnson, Jr., "*Débâcle sur la Seine* de Claude Monet: source du *Dégel à Briseville* d'Elstir," *Cahiers Marcel Proust*, n.s. 6. *Études proustiennes* (Paris, 1973), 1:163-176. I would like to thank Theodore Johnson for discussing his work on this subject with me. I am grateful to Marcel Muller for bringing this article to my attention. See also Thierry Laget, "Proust, peintre d'Elstir: Un catalogue irraisonné," *La Revue du Musée d'Orsay*, 48/14, no. 2 (February 1996): 71 (a copy of this article was kindly given to me by Henri Loyrette); and Caen, Abbaye aux Dames, *Les Figures d'Elstir: Proust et le peintre*, exh. cat., June 25-August 30, 1993, 54.

136 "Notre Exposition: Claude Monet," *La Vie Moderne* (June 19, 1880): 400.

137 The translations are those of Rewald 1984. For the letter of June 19, 1880 see *ibid*, 191; for the other letter, which Rewald dates to July 4, 1880, see *ibid*, 192.

138 Wildenstein 1974, 1:440, letter 191.

139 See Rivière 1921, 181, though he gets the apartment wrong; in 1880 it was on the rue Vintimille, rather than its earlier location on the rue Moncey.

140 As noted in Wildenstein 1974, 1:116.

141 See *ibid*, 1:350; *idem* 1996, 2:214.

142 See above, n. 51.

143 Levine 1976, 45, and Spate, 325, no. 36, thought that this review was probably written by Alfred de Lostalot. Bouillon *et al.*, 246, note that according to the *Grande Encyclopédie*, Lostalot's real name was Alfred de Bachoué.

144 "Concours et expositions," *La Chronique des Arts et de la Curiosité* 23 (June 12, 1880): 181.

145 Levine 1976, 25, 53-54, 62-64, 83-86; Bouillon *et al.*, 247; Levine 1994, 35-36, 69.

146 Levine 1976, 45.

147 Spate, 141 and n. 32, assumes that the painting referred to here was that in the Musée du Petit Palais; however this work was not in the *Vie Moderne* exhibition; see above p. 106.

148 See Levine 1976, 14-48, on the use of the concept.

149 In writings of Octave Mirbeau (see Levine 1976, 62) and of Lecomte (see Schiff, "The End of Impressionism," in San Francisco and Washington 1986, 66).

150 Silvestre, "Le Monde des Arts: Expositions particulières. Septième Exposition des artistes indépendants," *La Vie Moderne* (March 11, 1882): 150-151.

151 See James Kearns, "The writing on the wall: descriptions of painting in the art criticism of the French Symbolists," in *Artistic Relations: Literature and the Visual Arts in Nineteenth-Century France*, ed. Peter Collier and Robert Lethbridge (New Haven and London, 1994), 240, 244-247, 251; Levine 1994, esp. chaps. 11 and 12.

152 Levine 1976, 48.

153 Armand Sallanches, "L'Exposition des artistes indépendants," *Le Journal des Arts* (March 3, 1882): 1; the article is given in full in Berson, 412. The translation used here is found in San Francisco and Washington 1986, 402.

154 J[oris]-K[arl] Huysmans, "L'Exposition des Indépendants en 1880," in *idem*, *L'Art Moderne*, 2nd ed. (Paris 1902), 138.

155 "Appendice," in *idem* 1902, 292.

156 On the concept of emotion in Impressionist and Symbolist criticism, see Shiff, in San Francisco and Washington 1986, 65-66, 71, 74, 80-82.

157 Cézanne forwarded a copy of this letter to Zola at the artists' request; see above n. 42.

158 See above, n. 5.

Alphant, Marianne. *Claude Monet, une vie dans le paysage* (Paris, 1993).

Ann Arbor, The University of Michigan Museum of Art. *The Crisis of Impressionism, 1878-1882*, exh. cat. by Joel Isaacson, November 2, 1979–January 6, 1980 ([Ann Arbor], 1980).

Bortolatto, L. Rossi. *L'opera completa di Claude Monet, 1870-1889* (Milan, 1972).

Broude, Norma. *Impressionism, A Feminist Reading: The Gendering of Art, Science, and Nature in the Nineteenth Century* (New York, 1991).

Chicago, The Art Institute of Chicago. *Claude Monet 1840-1926*, exh. cat. by Charles F. Stuckey, July 22-November 26, 1995 (Chicago, 1995).

Duret, Théodore. "Claude Monet" [reprint of essay in brochure for exh. at *La Vie Moderne*, June 1880], in *idem*, *Critique d'avant-garde* (Paris, 1885).

__________. *Histoire des peintres impressionistes* (Paris, 1906).

Geoffroy, Gustave. *Claude Monet, sa vie, son temps, son oeuvre* (Paris, 1922).

Gordon, Robert, and Andrew Forge. *Monet* (New York, 1983).

House, John. *Monet: Nature into Art* (New Haven and London, 1986).

Isaacson, Joel. "*La Débâcle* by Claude Monet," *Bulletin, Museums of Art and Archaeology, The University of Michigan* 1 (1978): 1-15.

__________. *Observation and Reflection: Claude Monet* (Oxford, 1978).

Levine, Steven Z. *Monet and His Critics*, Ph.D. diss., Harvard University, 1974 (New York and London, 1976).

__________. *Monet, Narcissus, and Self-Reflection: The Modernist Myth of the Self* (Chicago and London, 1994).

London, Hayward Gallery, and Boston, Museum of Fine Arts. *Impressions of France: Monet, Renoir, Pissarro, and their Rivals*, exh. cat. by John House *et al.* (London, 1995).

New York, The Museum of Modern Art , and Los Angeles, Los Angeles County Museum. *Claude Monet. Seasons and Moments*, exh. cat. by William C. Seitz, Museum of Modern Art, March 9–May 15, 1960, Los Angeles County Museum, June 14–August 7, 1960 (Garden City, NY, 1960).

Paris, Réunion des musées nationaux. *Hommage à Claude Monet (1840-1926)*, exh. cat. by Hélène Adhémar *et al.*, Grand Palais, February 8-May 5, 1980 (Paris, 1980).

Rewald, John. *The History of Impressionism*, 4th rev. ed. (New York, 1973).

__________. *Post-Impressionism from Van Gogh to Gauguin*, 3rd ed., rev., (Boston, 1978).

Rewald, John, and Frances Weitzenhoffer, eds.. *Aspects of Monet: A Symposium on the Artist's Life and Times* (New York, 1984).

San Francisco, Fine Arts Museums of San Francisco, and Washington, DC, National Gallery of Art. *The New Painting, Impressionism 1874-1886*, exh. cat. by Charles S. Moffett *et al.*, 2nd ed. (San Francisco, 1986).

Seiberling, Grace. *Monet's Series*, Ph.D. diss., Yale University, 1976 (New York and London, 1981).

Spate, Virginia. *Claude Monet: Life and Work* (New York, 1992).

Stuckey, Charles F., *Monet: A Retrospective* (New York, 1985).

Tucker, Paul Hayes. *Claude Monet: Life and Art* (New Haven and London, 1995).

Venturi, Lionello. *Les Archives de l'Impressionisme: Lettres de Renoir, Monet, Pissarro, Sisley et autres. Mémoires de Paul Durand-Ruel. Documents*, 2 vols. (Paris and New York, 1939).

Washington, DC, The Phillips Collection. *Impressionists on the Seine: A Celebration of Renoir's Luncheon of the Boating Party*, exh. cat. by Eliza E. Rathbone *et al.*, September 21, 1996-February 9, 1997 (Washington, DC, 1996).

Wildenstein, Daniel. *Claude Monet: Biographie et catalogue raisonné*, 5 vols. (Lausanne, 1974-1991).

__________. *Monet: Catalogue raisonné, Werkverzeichnis*, trans. Chris Miller, Peter Snowdon, and Josephine Bacon, 4 vols. (Cologne, 1996).

PHOTOGRAPHY CREDITS

Cover
© University of Michigan Museum of Art, photo by Patrick J. Young.

Inside Front and Back Covers
Cartothèque IGN.

Frontispiece
Bibliothèque Historique de la Ville de Paris.

Color Plates
Cat. pl. 1 Kunstmuseum Bern, Bern; pl. 2 Dunedin Public Art Gallery, Dunedin, New Zealand; pl. 3 © University of Michigan Museum of Art, photo by Patrick J. Young; pl. 4 Fundación Colección Thyssen-Bornemisza, Madrid; pl. 5 © Photo RMN - Préveral; pls. 6, 11 The Metropolitan Museum of Art, New York; pl. 7 Dallas Museum of Art; pl. 8 Musée Marmottan, Paris; Photo: Giraudon; pl. 9 Art Gallery of Ontario, Toronto; pl. 10 © Photo RMN - Jean; pl. 12 The Minneapolis Institute of Arts, Minneapolis, Minnesota.

Stuckey
Fig. 1 Copyright © The British Museum, London; fig. 2 Courtesy of the Trustees, The National Gallery, London; fig. 3 Musée des Beaux-Arts, Tours; fig. 4 Kimbell Art Museum, Forth Worth, Texas; fig. 5 Photograph © 1997 The Museum of Modern Art, New York; fig. 6 Fine Arts Museum, Budapest; figs. 7, 8, 10 © Photo RMN; fig. 9 National Gallery of Victoria, Melbourne, Australia.

McNamara
Fig. 1 Cartothèque IGN; fig. 2 Bibliothèque Nationale, Paris, Photo: Lhomel; fig. 3 National Gallery of Scotland; fig. 4 © Photo Carole McNamara; fig. 5 Bibliothèque Nationale, Paris; fig. 6 © Rouen, Musée des Beaux-Arts. Photo: Didier Tragin, Catherine Lancier; fig. 7 Foundation E.G. Bürhle Collection, Zürich; fig. 8 © Photo RMN - H. Lewandowski; fig. 9 Roger-Viollet, Paris; fig. 10 Musée Marmottan, Paris. Photo: Giraudon; figs. 11, 12, 13 Courtesy of the Archives of the Wildenstein Institute, Paris; figs. 14, 15, 16, 17, 18, 19, 20, 21, 22, 23, 24, 25, 26 © University of Michigan Museum of Art; photos by Patrick J. Young.

Dixon
Fig. 1 Shelburne Museum, Shelburne, Vermont, Photograph by Ken Burris; fig. 2 © Photothèque des Musées de la Ville de Paris, Photographer: P. Pierrain; fig. 3 Photograph © 1996, The Art Institute of Chicago. All Rights Reserved; fig. 4 Joslyn Art Museum, Omaha, Nebraska; fig. 5 Musée Marmottan, Paris. Photo: Giraudon.